Rick Steves®

POCKET
PRAGUE

Rick Steves & Honza Vihan
with Gene Openshaw

Contents

Introduction

Few cities can match Prague's over-the-top romance, evocative Old World charm...and tourist crowds. Residents call their town "Praha" (PRAH-hah). It's big, with about 1.3 million people. But during a quick visit, you'll focus on its relatively compact old center.

Prague is equal parts historic and fun. As the only Central European capital to escape the large-scale bombing of the last century's wars, it's one of Europe's best-preserved cities. It's a city of willowy Art Nouveau facades, Mozart concerts, and some of the best beer in Europe. Wind through walkable neighborhoods, cross the famous statue-lined Charles Bridge, and hike up to the world's biggest castle for sweeping views of the city's spires and domes. You'll see rich remnants of the city's strong Jewish heritage and stark reminders of the communist era. And you'll meet today's vibrant mix of locals and expats. Prague itself seems a work of art.

Introduction

Prague

400 Meters
400 Yards

Královský Letohrádek

Pražský Hrad

JELENÍ

← To Brusnice & Pohořelec

MARIÁNSKÉ HRADBY

ROYAL SUMMER PALACE

Tram #22

Chotkovy Park

CHOTKOVA

NA OPYŠI

U BRUSKÝCH KASÁREN

NÁBŘEŽÍ EDVARDA BENEŠE

Royal Gardens

CASTLE QUARTER

GOLDEN LANE & TOY MUSEUM

STARÉ ZÁMECKÉ SCHODY

KLÁROV

Jelení Příkop

KATEDRÁLA SV. VÍTA

Pálffy Gardens

Fürstenberg Gardens

Malo-stranská

Malo-stranská

NÁRODNÍ GALERIE

PRAGUE CASTLE

VALDŠTEJNSKÁ

WWII MONUMENT

KOSÁRKOVO NÁBŘEŽÍ

Vltava

RUDOLFINUM

Na Valech Gardens

TOMÁŠSKÁ

Wallenstein Pal. Gdn.

MÁNESŮV MOST

Castle Square

ZÁMECKÉ SCHODY

THUNOVSKÁ

LETENSKÁ

Vojanovy Gardens

U LUŽICKÉHO SEMINÁŘE

CIHELNÁ

ALŠOVO NÁBŘEŽÍ

KE HRADU

ÚVOZ

NERUDOVA

MALOSTRANSKÉ NÁM.

JOSEFSKÁ

MOSTECKÁ

MÍŠEŇSKÁ

BŘETISLAVOVA

ST. NICHOLAS

SV. FRANTIŠEK Z ASSISI

VLAŠSKÁ

VLAŠSKÁ

TRŽIŠTĚ

PROKOPSKÁ NEBOVIDSKÁ

SASKÁ

LÁZEŇSKÁ

KARLŮV MOST

BRIDGE TOWER

LITTLE QUARTER

LENNON WALL

CHARLES BRIDGE

ANENSKÁ

Lobkovická Zahrada

KOSTEL PANNY MARIE VÍTĚZNÉ

HARANTOVA

Tram #22

KARMELITSKÁ

NA KAMPĚ

SMETANA MUSEUM

PETŘÍN TOWER

Seminářská Zahrada

HELLICHOVA

PELCLOVA

Kampa Island

NÁRODNÍ DIVADLO

SMETANOVO NÁBŘEŽÍ

HELLICHOVA

Petřín Park

Střelecký Island

Národní Divadlo

MOST LEGIÍ

NATIONAL THEATER

ZOFIN

Slovanský Island

MASARYKOVO NÁBŘEŽÍ

MAP LEGEND

Ⓜ	Metro Stop	🏛	Church
Ⓑ	Bus Stop		Synagogue
Ⓣ	Taxi Stand		Park
▪	Point of Interest	●	Fountain
↑	Entrance		Pedestrian Zone
WC	Restroom		Stairs
	View Point	-----	Walk/Tour Route
	Tourist Info	------	Railway

Use this legend to help you navigate the maps in this book.

Ⓝ

Rick Steves | Pocket Prague

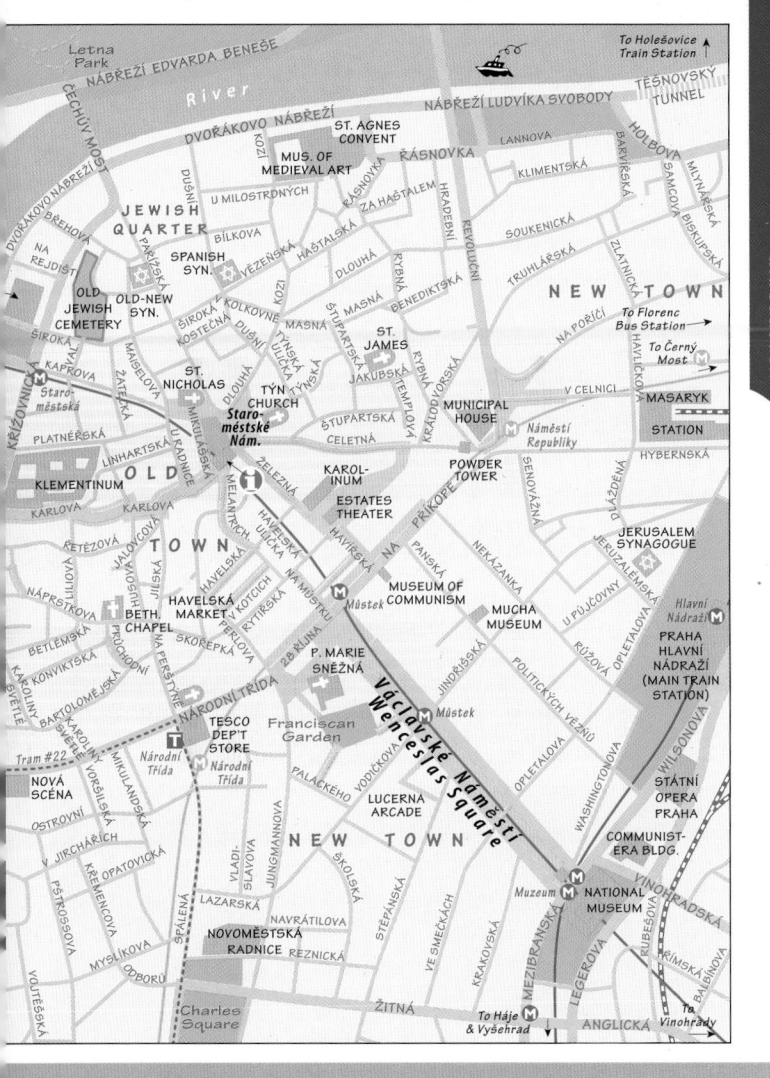

Key to This Book

Sights are rated:

▲▲▲ **Don't miss**

▲▲ **Try hard to see**

▲ **Worthwhile if you can make it**

No rating **Worth knowing about**

Tourist information offices are abbreviated as **TI** and bathrooms are **WCs**.

Like Europe, this book uses the **24-hour clock.** It's the same through 12:00 noon, then keep going: 13:00 (1:00 p.m.), 14:00 (2:00 p.m.), and so on. For opening times, if a sight is listed as "May–Oct daily 9:00–16:00," it's open from 9 a.m. until 4 p.m. from the first day of May until the last day of October.

About This Book

With this book, I've selected only the best of Prague—admittedly, a tough call. The core of the book is five self-guided walks and tours that show off the region's greatest sights and experiences. My Prague Old Town Walk—from the Old Town Square to the historic Charles Bridge—introduces you to the city and its main sights. The Jewish Quarter Tour leads through the synagogues and museums of Europe's best-preserved former Jewish ghetto. The Wenceslas Square Walk shows off the glitzier New Town, and recalls Prague's tumultuous years under communist rule and its exciting liberation in the 1989 Velvet Revolution. The Prague Castle Tour focuses on

Prague's center is pedestrian-friendly.

Carriages and walkers rule the roads.

only the most important of the many sights in this historic complex, including the towering St. Vitus Cathedral. And the *Slav Epic* Tour presents the poignant story of the Slavic people through the impressive canvases by the greatest modern Czech artist, Alfons Mucha.

The rest of the book is a traveler's tool kit. You'll find plenty more about the area's attractions, from shopping to nightlife to less touristy sights. And there are helpful hints on saving money, avoiding crowds, getting around on public transit, finding a great meal, and much more.

If you'd like more information than this Pocket Guide offers, I've sprinkled the book liberally with web references. For general travel tips—as well as updates for this book—see www.ricksteves.com.

Prague by Neighborhood

The Vltava River divides the city in two. East of the river are the Old Town and New Town, the Main Train Station, and most of the recommended hotels. To the west of the river is Prague Castle, and below that, the sleepy Little Quarter. Connecting the two halves are several bridges, including the landmark Charles Bridge.

Think of Prague as a collection of neighborhoods. In fact, until about 1800, Prague actually was four distinct towns with four distinct personalities.

Old Town (Staré Město): Nestled in the bend of the river, this is the historic core, where most tourists spend their time. It's pedestrian-friendly, with small winding streets, old buildings, shops, and beer halls and cafés. In the center sits the charming Old Town Square. Slicing east-west through the Old Town is the main pedestrian axis, along Celetná and Karlova streets.

Within the Old Town, tucked closest to the river, is the **Jewish Quarter (Josefov),** a several-block area with sights from Prague's deep Jewish heritage. It also holds the city's glitziest shopping area.

New Town (Nové Město): Stretching south from the Old Town is the long, broad expanse of Wenceslas Square, marking the center of the New Town. As the name implies, it's the neighborhood for modern buildings, fancy department stores, and a few communist-era sights.

Castle Quarter (Hradčany): High atop a hill on the west side of the river stands the massive complex of Prague Castle, marked by the spires of St. Vitus Cathedral. The surrounding area is noble and leafy, with grand buildings, little commerce, and few pubs.

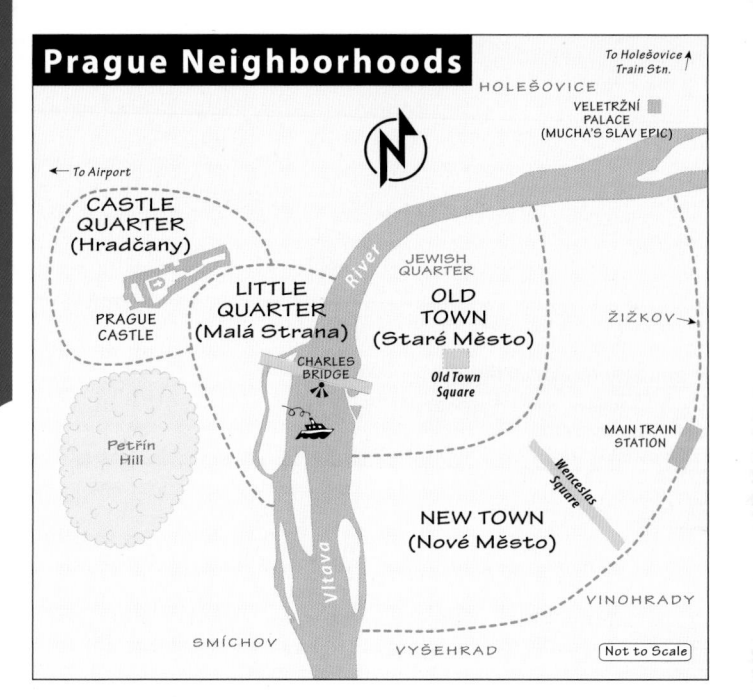

Prague Neighborhoods

To Holešovice
Train Stn.

HOLEŠOVICE

VELETRŽNÍ
PALACE
(MUCHA'S SLAV EPIC)

← To Airport

CASTLE
QUARTER
(Hradčany)

PRAGUE
CASTLE

LITTLE
QUARTER
(Malá Strana)

JEWISH
QUARTER

OLD
TOWN
(Staré Město)

ŽIŽKOV

CHARLES
BRIDGE

Old Town
Square

Petřín
Hill

MAIN TRAIN
STATION

Wenceslas
Square

NEW TOWN
(Nové Město)

Vltava
River

VINOHRADY

SMÍCHOV

VYŠEHRAD

Not to Scale

Little Quarter (Malá Strana): Nestled at the foot of Castle Hill is this pleasant former town of fine palaces and gardens (and several minor sights).

Away from the Center: A short ride away on public transit, you'll find important sights like the *Slav Epic* and the Vyšehrad park.

Planning Your Time

The following day-plans give you an idea of how much an organized, motivated, and caffeinated person can see. Prague deserves at least two full sightseeing days, and you might consider other side-trips.

Day 1: Take my Old Town Walk to get oriented to the city's core. Have lunch in the Old Town or Little Quarter. Explore the Little Quarter. In the midafternoon, follow my Jewish Quarter Tour. In the evening (tonight or

Daily Reminder

Sunday: St. Vitus Cathedral at Prague Castle is closed Sunday morning for Mass. Some stores are closed.

Monday: Mucha's *Slav Epic* and the Museum of Medieval Art are closed. Most of the other major sights are open. Some lesser sights are closed, including Týn Church and the Church of St. James.

Tuesday-Friday: All sights are open.

Saturday: The Jewish Quarter sights are closed.

other nights), consider a classical concert, a beer hall, pop music, or Black Light Theater.

Day 2: Leave your hotel by 8:00 to be at St. Vitus Cathedral when it opens at 9:00, then follow my Prague Castle Tour. As you leave the castle, tour Lobkowicz Palace. Have lunch in the Little Quarter, below the castle. Ride the tram to see Mucha's *Slav Epic*. Tram back to town and follow my New Town Walk. Tour the Mucha Museum (unless you're already Mucha-ed out).

Day 3: Choose from any number of museums (see the Sights chapter for ideas), such as the Museum of Medieval Art, the Heydrich Terror memorial, the Museum of Communism, or ascend the Old Town Hall tower for views.

With More Time: Consider a day trip to Kutná Hora, Terezín, or Karlštejn Castle (see page 136).

These are busy day-plans, so be sure to schedule in slack time for

Prague is a city of quaint neighborhoods.

The Old Town Square is the historic center.

Prague at a Glance

Prague is a fine place to wander around and just take in the fun atmosphere. Plan some worthwhile activities—take a self-guided tram tour (page 126), hire a local guide (page 180), enjoy a concert (page 178), or go for a scenic paddle on the river (page 125).

In the Old Town

▲▲▲**Old Town Square** Magical main square of Old World Prague, with dozens of colorful facades, the dramatic Jan Hus Memorial, looming Týn Church, and fanciful Astronomical Clock. **Hours:** Týn Church generally open to sightseers Tue-Sat 10:00-13:00 & 15:00-17:00, Sun 10:30-12:00, closed Mon; clock strikes on the hour daily 9:00-21:00, until 20:00 in winter; clock tower open Tue-Sun 9:00-21:00, Mon 11:00-21:00. See page 17.

▲▲▲**Charles Bridge** An atmospheric, statue-lined bridge that connects the Old Town to the Little Quarter and Prague Castle. **Hours:** Always open and crossable. See page 38.

▲▲▲**Jewish Quarter** The finest collection of Jewish sights in Europe, featuring various synagogues and an evocative cemetery. **Hours:** Most sights open April-Oct Sun-Fri 9:00-18:00, Nov-March until 17:00, closed Sat and Jewish holidays. See page 41.

▲▲**Museum of Medieval Art** The best Gothic art in the country, at the former Convent of St. Agnes. **Hours:** Tue-Sun 10:00-18:00, closed Mon, may close sporadically due to budget cuts. See page 118.

▲**Havelská Market** Colorful open-air market that sells crafts and produce. **Hours:** Daily 9:00-18:00. See page 34.

▲**Klementinum** National Library's lavish Baroque Hall and Observatory Tower (with views), open by 45-minute tour only. **Hours:** Tours depart daily every half-hour 10:00-17:30, shorter hours off-season. See page 116.

In the New Town

▲▲**Wenceslas Square** Lively boulevard at the heart of modern Prague. **Hours:** Always open. See page 62.

▲▲**Mucha Museum** Easy-to-appreciate collection of Art Nouveau works by Czech artist Alfons Mucha. **Hours:** Daily 10:00-18:00. See page 121.

Introduction

▲▲**Municipal House** Pure Art Nouveau architecture, including Prague's largest concert hall and several eateries. **Hours:** Daily 10:00-18:00. See page 29.

▲**Museum of Communism** The rise and fall of the regime, from start to Velvet finish. **Hours:** Daily 9:00-21:00. See page 122.

▲**National Memorial to the Heroes of the Heydrich Terror** Tribute to members of the resistance, who assassinated a notorious Nazi architect of the Holocaust. **Hours:** Tue-Sun 9:00-17:00, closed Mon. See page 127.

In the Little Quarter

▲**Petřín Hill** Little Quarter hill with public art, a funicular, and a replica of the Eiffel Tower. **Hours:** Funicular—daily 8:00-22:00; tower—daily 10:00-22:00, shorter hours off-season. See page 131.

In the Castle Quarter

▲▲▲**St. Vitus Cathedral** The Czech Republic's most important church, featuring a climbable tower and striking stained-glass windows. **Hours:** Daily April-Oct 9:00-17:00, Nov-March 9:00-16:00, closed Sunday mornings year-round for Mass. See page 80.

▲▲**Prague Castle** Traditional seat of Czech rulers, with St. Vitus Cathedral (see above), Old Royal Palace, Basilica of St. George, and shop-lined Golden Lane. **Hours:** Castle sights—daily April-Oct 9:00-17:00, Nov-March 9:00-16:00; castle grounds—daily 5:00-24:00. See page 73.

▲▲**Lobkowicz Palace** The most entertaining palace in town. **Hours:** Daily 10:00-18:00. See page 132.

▲**Strahov Monastery and Library** Baroque center of learning, with ornate reading rooms and old-fashioned science exhibits. **Hours:** Daily 9:00-11:45 & 13:00-17:00. See page 133.

Outside the Center

▲▲▲*Slav Epic* Alfons Mucha's 20 enormous canvases at Veletržní Palace depicting momentous events of Slavic history. **Hours:** Tue-Sun 10:00-18:00, closed Mon. See page 95.

▲**Vyšehrad** Welcoming, untouristy park at the site of a former hilltop palace, rich with Czech history and great city views. **Hours:** Park always open, though various sights inside (church, cemetery, etc.) close at 18:00 (17:00 off-season). See page 135.

Official Name: It's the Česká Republika, born on January 1, 1993, along with Slovakia, when the nation of Czechoslovakia—formed after World War I and dominated by the USSR after World War II—split into two countries.

Population: 10.6 million people. About 64 percent are ethnic Czechs, who speak Czech. One in 10 is Roman Catholic, but the majority (55 percent) list their religion as unaffiliated.

Latitude and Longitude: 50°N and 15°E (similar latitude to Vancouver, British Columbia).

Area: 31,000 square miles (similar to South Carolina or Maine).

Geography: The Czech Republic comprises three regions—Bohemia (Čechy), Moravia (Morava), and a small slice of Silesia (Slezsko). The climate is generally cool and partly cloudy.

Biggest Cities: Prague (the capital, 1.3 million), Brno (370,000), Ostrava (300,000), and Plzeň (168,000).

Economy: The gross domestic product equals about $286 billion (similar to Indiana). The GDP per capita is approximately $26,300, half that of the average American. Major moneymakers for the country include machine parts, cars and trucks, and beer—Pilsner Urquell and the original Budweiser. The vast majority of Czech beer is consumed domestically. More than a third of trade is with next-door-neighbor Germany.

Currency: 20 Czech crowns (*koruna*, Kč) = about $1.

Government: From 1948 to 1989, Czechoslovakia was a communist state under Soviet control. Today, the Czech Republic is a member of the European Union and a strong democracy. Its parliament is made up of 200 representatives elected every four years and 81 senators elected for six years. The president is selected every five years by popular vote.

Flag: The Czech flag is red (bottom), white (top), and blue (a triangle along the hoist side).

The Average Czech: The average Czech has 1.4 kids (slowly rising after the sharp decline that followed the end of communism), will live 78 years, and has one television in the house.

picnics, laundry, people-watching, leisurely dinners, concerts, shopping, fine Pilsner, and recharging your touristic batteries. Slow down and be open to unexpected experiences and the courtesy of the Czech people.

Quick Tips: Book hotel rooms as far in advance as possible, especially for May, June, and September. Get comfortable with Prague's excellent tram system. Take advantage of my free audio-tour of the Prague City Walk from Wenceslas Square to the Charles Bridge (see page 181). Plan your sightseeing at Prague Castle to avoid the horrendous crowds from midmorning through early afternoon. Jewish Quarter sights close on Saturday and Jewish holidays, and some museums are closed on Monday.

And finally, remember that—although Prague's sights can be crowded and stressful—the city itself is all about gentility and grace, so...be flexible. And have a terrific trip!

Co-authors Rick Steves (right) and Honza Vihan (center) enjoy a traditional meal (which often includes beer) with a happy local.

Old Town Walk

A boomtown since the 10th century, Prague's compact, pedestrian-friendly Old Town has long been a busy commercial quarter, filled with merchants, guilds, and supporters of the Church reformer Jan Hus (who wanted a Czech-style Catholicism). Today it's Prague's tourism ground zero, jammed with tasteful landmarks and tacky amusements alike.

This walk starts in the heart of the neighborhood, the Old Town Square. From here we'll snake through the surrounding neighborhood, get a glimpse of the New Town (at Wenceslas Square), and end at the river, on the Charles Bridge—one of the most atmospheric spots in all of Europe. Along the way, we'll see Baroque statues, Art Nouveau facades, and a curious old clock. And we'll learn the story of how the Czech people have courageously fought against foreign oppression, from Habsburgs to Nazis to Soviet communists.

ORIENTATION

Length of This Walk: Allow two to three hours for this walk. It's a great overview of sights you may want to visit in depth later.

When to Go: The Old Town Square and surrounding streets are packed midday, and never really quiet. A huge bottleneck occurs in front of the Astronomical Clock near the top of each hour, but as soon as the show's over, the tourists disperse quickly.

Getting There: This walk begins right on the Old Town Square, Prague's centerpiece.

Týn Church: 30-Kč requested donation, generally open to sightseers Tue-Sat 10:00-13:00 & 15:00-17:00, Sun 10:30-12:00, closed Mon.

Town Hall Tower: 110 Kč, Tue-Sun 9:00-21:00, Mon 11:00-21:00.

Church of St. James: Free, Tue-Sun 9:30-12:00 & 14:00-16:00, closed Mon.

Municipal House: Free to view entrance halls and public spaces; daily 10:00-18:00; tours—290 Kč, usually 3/day, leaving between 11:00 and 17:00; 55 Kč extra to take photos.

Museum of Communism: 190 Kč, daily 9:00-21:00.

Havelská Market: Open-air market open daily 9:00-18:00, produce best on weekdays; more souvenirs, puppets, and toys on weekends.

Klementinum: Tour—220 Kč, departs daily every half-hour 10:00-17:30; shorter hours off-season.

Charles Bridge Tower Climb: 90 Kč, April-Sept daily 10:00-22:00, March and Oct until 20:00, Nov-Feb until 18:00.

Services: Pay WCs are common throughout Prague's Old Town; for example, in the Old Town Hall or at the square's Kotleta Restaurant.

Starring: Prague's showpiece main square, fine old churches, architectural landmarks, and the spunky Czech spirit.

THE TOUR BEGINS

▶ *Plant yourself anywhere in the Old Town Square, and survey the scene.*

Old Town Square

Take in the essence of modern Prague, a city of 1.3 million people and the capital of the Czech Republic. The vast square is ringed with colorful buildings; dotted with towers, steeples, and statues; lined with cafés; and alive with people. Street performers provide a constant soundtrack. Horse carriages and Segways zip through constantly—a reminder that Prague is as much a city of yesterday as a city of today.

This has been a market square since the 11th century. It became the nucleus of the Old Town (or Staré Město) in the 13th century, when its Town Hall was built. In past times, it would have been the site of commerce, parades, demonstrations, and executions. Today, the old-time market stalls have been replaced by outdoor cafés and the tackiest breed of souvenir stands. But under this shallow surface, the square hides a magic power to evoke the history that has passed through here.

▶ *Begin with the square's centerpiece, the...*

❶ Memorial to Jan Hus

This monument is an enduring icon of the long struggle for Czech freedom. In the center, Jan Hus—the religious reformer who has become a symbol of Czech nationalism—stands tall. Hus, born in 1369, was a Prague priest who stood up to both the Catholic Church and the Austrian Habsburg oppressors. His defiant stance—as depicted so powerfully in

The Old Town Square still feels old.

Jan Hus, symbol of Czech nationalism

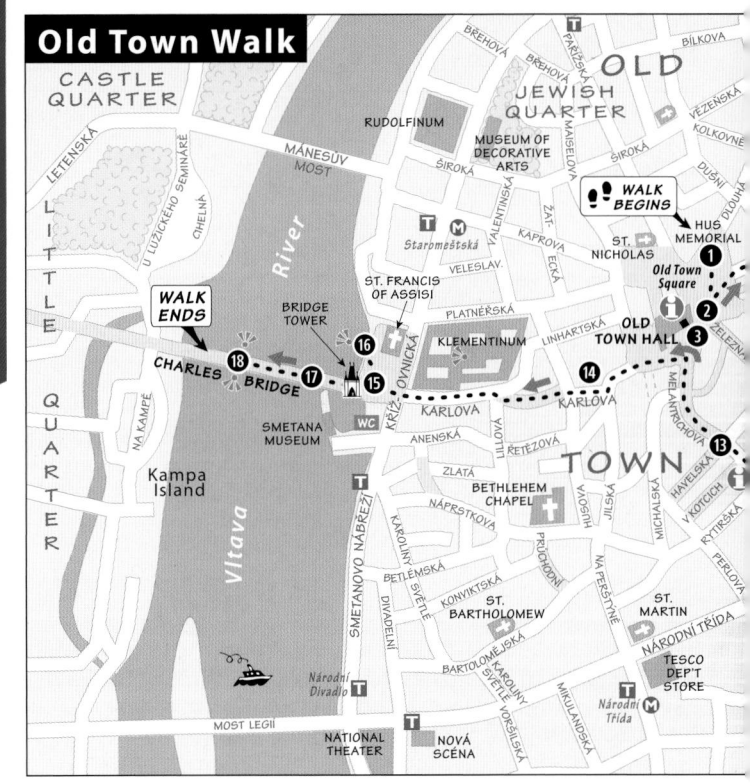

Old Town Walk

CASTLE QUARTER

OLD JEWISH QUARTER

RUDOLFINUM

MUSEUM OF DECORATIVE ARTS

MÁNESŮV MOST

WALK BEGINS

ST. NICHOLAS

HUS MEMORIAL ❶

Old Town Square

Staroměstská

WALK ENDS

BRIDGE TOWER

ST. FRANCIS OF ASSISI

KLEMENTINUM

OLD TOWN HALL ❸

❷

CHARLES BRIDGE ❶❽ ❶❼ ❶❻ ❶❺

KARLOVA ❶❹

❶❸

SMETANA MUSEUM

WC

TOWN

Kampa Island

BETHLEHEM CHAPEL

Vltava

ST. BARTHOLOMEW

ST. MARTIN

NÁRODNÍ TŘÍDA

TESCO DEP'T STORE

Národní Třída

Národní Divadlo

MOST LEGIÍ

NATIONAL THEATER

NOVÁ SCÉNA

this monument—galvanized the Czech people, who rallied to fight not just for their religious beliefs but for independence from foreign control.

But Hus was about a century ahead of his time. He was arrested, charged with heresy, excommunicated, and, in 1415, burned at the stake. His followers picked up the torch and fought on for two decades in the Hussite Wars, which killed tens of thousands and left Bohemia a virtual wasteland.

Surrounding Hus' statue are the Hussite followers who battled the Habsburgs. One patriot holds a cup, or chalice. This symbolizes one of

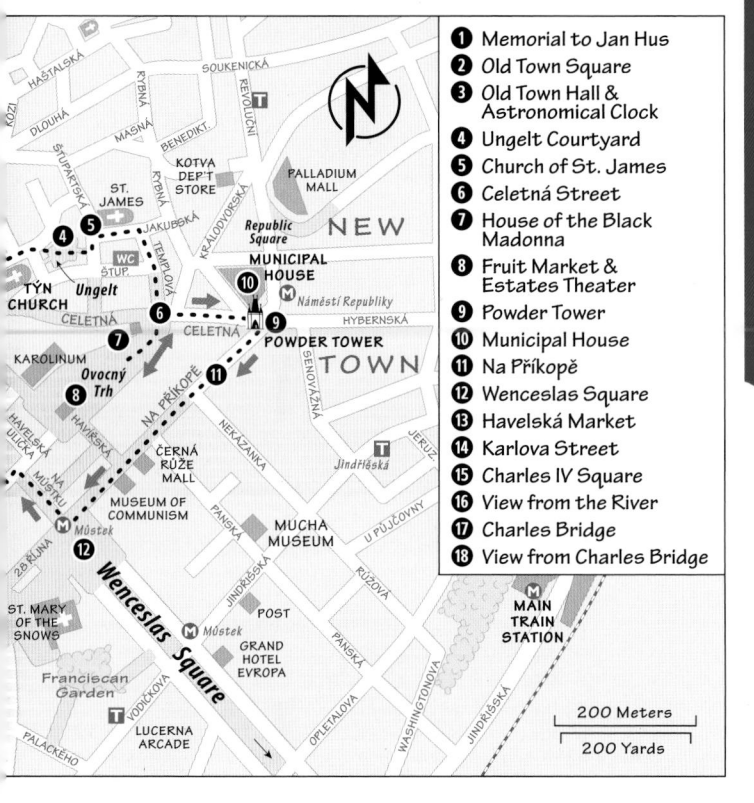

1. Memorial to Jan Hus
2. Old Town Square
3. Old Town Hall & Astronomical Clock
4. Ungelt Courtyard
5. Church of St. James
6. Celetná Street
7. House of the Black Madonna
8. Fruit Market & Estates Theater
9. Powder Tower
10. Municipal House
11. Na Příkopě
12. Wenceslas Square
13. Havelská Market
14. Karlova Street
15. Charles IV Square
16. View from the River
17. Charles Bridge
18. View from Charles Bridge

the changes the Hussites were fighting for: the right of everyone (not just priests) to drink the wine at Communion. Look into the survivors' faces—it was a bitter fight. In 1620, their rebellious cause was brutally crushed by the Catholic Habsburgs at the pivotal Battle of White Mountain fought outside Prague—effectively ending Czech independence for three centuries.

As we'll see on this walk, Jan Hus was the linchpin in Czech history. Before him was the Golden Age of great kings (c. 1200-1400). After him came centuries of foreign domination. But the story ends well. Huddled just behind Jan Hus are a mother and her children—representing the ultimate rebirth of the Czech nation.

Each subsequent age has interpreted Hus to its liking: For Protestants, Hus was the founder of the first Protestant church (though he was actually an ardent Catholic); for revolutionaries, this critic of the Church's power was a proponent of social equality; for nationalists, this Czech preacher was the defender of the language; and for communists, Hus was the first ideologue to preach the gospel of socialism. But regardless of who was in power, Hus' importance to the Czech people has never wavered.

▶ *Stepping away from the Hus Memorial, stand in the center of the Old Town Square, and take a 360-degree...*

❷ Old Town Square Orientation Spin-Tour

Whirl clockwise to get a look at Prague's diverse architectural styles: Gothic, Renaissance, Baroque, Rococo, and Art Nouveau. Remember, Prague was largely spared the devastating aerial bombardments of World War II that leveled so many European cities (like Berlin, Warsaw, and Budapest). Few places can match the Old Town Square for Old World charm.

Start with the green domes of the Baroque **Church of St. Nicholas.** Originally Catholic, now Hussite, this church is a popular venue for concerts. The Jewish Quarter is a few blocks behind the church, down the uniquely tree-lined "Paris Street" (Pařížská)—which also has the best line-up of Art Nouveau houses in Prague, and arguably in all of Europe.

Spin to the right. Behind the Hus Memorial is a fine yellow building that introduces us to Prague's wonderful world of Art Nouveau: pastel colors, fanciful stonework, wrought-iron balconies, colorful murals—and what are those statues on top doing? Prague's architecture is a wonderland of ornamental details.

Continue spinning a few doors to the right to the large, red-and-tan Rococo **Kinský Palace,** which displays the National Gallery's Asian arts collection (and has a handy WC in the courtyard).

Farther to the right is the towering, Gothic **Týn Church** (pronounced "teen"), with its fanciful twin spires. It's been the Old Town's leading church in every era. In medieval times, it was Catholic. When the Hussites took power (c. 1420-1620), they made it the headquarters of their faith. After the Hussite defeat, the Habsburgs returned it to Catholicism. The symbolism tells the story: Between the church's two towers, find a golden medallion

Týn Church's towers are a symbol of the city.

of the Virgin Mary. Beneath that is a niche—now empty. But in Hussite times, a golden chalice stood there, symbolizing their cause. When the Catholics triumphed, they melted down the chalice and made it into this golden image of Mary. The church interior (described on page 115) is uncharacteristically bright for a Gothic building because of its clear Baroque windowpanes and whitewash.

The row of pastel houses in front of Týn Church has a mixture of Gothic, Renaissance, and Baroque facades. If you like live music, check out the convenient **Via Musica box office** near the church's front door to find out all your options (see page 178); we'll pass it later on this walk.

Spinning right, to the south side of the square, take in more **glorious facades,** each a different color with a different gable on top—step gables, triangular, bell-shaped. The tan house at #16 has a steepled bay window and a mural of St. Wenceslas on horseback, and Albert Einstein once lectured at the light-orange house at #18.

Finally, you reach the pointed 250-foot-tall spire marking the 14th-century **Old Town Hall.** The tower is Neo-Gothic.

Approach the Old Town Hall. At the base of the tower, near the corner of the tree-filled park, find **27 white crosses** inlaid in the pavement. These mark the spot where 27 Protestant nobles, merchants, and intellectuals were beheaded in 1621 after the Battle of White Mountain—still one of the grimmest chapters in the country's history.

▶ *Around the left side of the tower are two big, fancy, old clock faces, being admired by many, many tourists.*

❸ Old Town Hall and Astronomical Clock

The Old Town Hall, with its distinctive trapezoidal tower, was built in the 1350s, during Prague's Golden Age. Check out the ornately carved Gothic entrance door to the left of the clock; a bit farther to the left is another door, leading to the TI, public pay WC, and ticket desk for riding the elevator up to the top of the clock tower, or touring the interior of the Old Town Hall (both described on page 114).

But for now, turn your attention to that famous **Astronomical Clock.** See if you can figure out how it works. Of the two giant dials on the tower, the top one tells the time. It has a complex series of revolving wheels within wheels, but the basics are simple:

The two big, outer dials tell the time in a 24-hour circle. Of these, the inner dial is stationary and is marked with the Roman numerals I-XII twice, starting at the top and bottom of the dial—noon and midnight. The colorful background of this dial indicates the amount of daylight at different times of day: The black circle surrounded by orange at the bottom half (from XII "p.m." to IV "a.m.") is nighttime, while the blue top half is daytime, and the shades of gray and orange between them represent dawn and dusk.

Meanwhile, the outer dial (with the golden numbers on a black band) lists the numbers 1 through 24, in a strange but readable Bohemian script. But because this uses the medieval Italian method of telling time—where the day resets at sunset—the 1 is not at the top, but somewhere in the lower-right quadrant of the Roman dial. The Roman numeral that the Bohemian 1 lines up with tells you the time of last night's sunset (typically between IV and VIII "p.m.").

The "big hand" (with the golden sun on it) does one slow sweep each 24-hour period, marking the time on both dials.

Now pay attention to the offset inner ring, marked with the zodiac signs. This ring both rotates on its own, and moves around the outer dial, so the sunny "big hand" also lands on today's zodiac sign. And the "little

Ponder the wheels-within-wheels and intriguing artwork of the fascinating Astronomical Clock.

A Little Walking History

As you're walking through living Czech history, you'll note a theme that runs throughout: how the tiny Czech nation has had to constantly fight to survive amid more powerful neighbors.

The nation was born under the duke Wenceslas, who unified the Czech people 1,100 years ago. Prague's medieval Golden Age peaked under Charles IV (c. 1350), who built many of the city's best-known monuments.

Over the next centuries, the Czechs were forever struggling to maintain their proud heritage. First, they defied the pope, led by religious reformer Jan Hus. Then they chafed under the yoke of the Austrian Habsburgs. Finally, in the historic year 1918, the modern nation of Czechoslovakia was created. Unfortunately, that nation was trampled yet again—first by Nazis, then by the communist Soviet Union. In 1989, huge protests peacefully tossed out the communists in the Velvet Revolution. In the 1990s, the Czechs and Slovaks amicably split in the Velvet Divorce. Now in the 21st century, the Czech Republic has fully joined the community of nations as a free and independent people.

hand" (with a blue moon) appears in this month's zodiac—is the moon in Taurus?

If all this seems complex to us, it must have been a marvel in the early 1400s, when the clock was installed. Remember that back then, everything revolved around the Earth (the fixed middle background—with Prague marking the center, of course). The clock was heavily damaged during World War II, and much of what you see today is a reconstruction.

The second dial, below the clock, was added in the 19th century. It shows the signs of the zodiac, scenes from the seasons of a rural peasant's life, and a ring of saints' names. There's one for each day of the year, and a marker on top indicates today's special saint. In the center is a castle, symbolizing Prague.

Four statues flank the upper clock. These politically incorrect symbols evoke a 15th-century outlook: The figure staring into a mirror stands for vanity, a Jewish moneylender holding a bag of coins is greed, and (on the right side) a Turk with a mandolin symbolizes hedonism. All these worldly goals are vain in the face of Death, whose hourglass reminds us that our time is unavoidably running out.

The clock strikes the top of the hour and puts on a little glockenspiel show daily from 9:00 to 21:00 (until 20:00 in winter). As the hour approaches, keep your eye on Death. First, Death tips his hourglass and pulls the cord, ringing the bell, while the moneylender jingles his purse. Then the windows open and the 12 apostles shuffle past, acknowledging the gang of onlookers. Finally the rooster at the very top crows and the hour is rung. The hour is often wrong because of Daylight Saving Time (completely senseless to 15th-century clockmakers). I find an alternative view just as interesting: As the cock crows, face the crowd and snap a photo of the mass of gaping tourists.

Before moving on, stand at the Astronomical Clock and get oriented. You're at the axis of several main streets. To the right and left are Celetná and Karlova streets, which form the main east-west spine through the Old Town. Behind you is Melantrichova street, which leads south to Wenceslas Square. We'll be traversing all of these on our walk.

▶ *Let's leave the Old Town Square. Our next stop is directly behind the Týn Church: Cross through the square and head down the street along the left side of the church (Týnská) for about 100 yards, passing the convenient* **Via Musica box office.**

Continue straight, then enter the sturdy gate into a courtyard called...

❹ Ungelt

This pleasant, cobbled, quiet courtyard of upscale restaurants and shops is one of the Old Town's oldest places. During the Bohemian Golden Age (c. 1200-1400), it was a cosmopolitan center of international trade. Prague—located at the geographical center of Europe—attracted Germans selling furs, Italians selling fine art, Frenchmen selling cloth, and Arabs selling spices. They converged on this courtyard, where they could store their goods and pay their customs (which is what *Ungelt* means, in German). In return, the king granted them protection, housing, and a stable

Ungelt courtyard, for medieval merchants

St. James, the Old Town's best interior

for their horses. By day, they'd sell their wares on the Old Town Square. At night, they'd return here to drink and exchange news from their native lands. Notice that, to protect the goods, there are only two entrances to the complex. After centuries of disuse, the Ungelt has been marvelously restored—a great place for dinner, and a reminder that Prague has been a cosmopolitan center for most of its history.

► *Exit the Ungelt at the far end. Just to your left, across the street, is the...*

⑤ Church of St. James (Kostel Sv. Jakuba)

With perhaps the most beautiful church interior in the Old Town, the Church of St. James has been the home of the Minorite Order almost as long as merchants have occupied Ungelt. A medieval city was a complex phenomenon: Commerce, prostitution, and a life of contemplation existed side by side. (I guess it's not that much different from today.)

Step inside (or, if it's locked, peek through the glass door). Artistically, St. James is a stunning example of how simple medieval spaces could be rebuilt into sumptuous feasts of Baroque decoration. The original interior was destroyed by fire in 1689; what's here now is an early 18th-century remodel. The blue light in the altar highlights one of Prague's most venerated treasures—the bejeweled Madonna Pietatis. Above the *pietà,* as if held aloft by hummingbird-like angels, is a painting of the martyrdom of St. James.

Proceed grandly up the central aisle, enjoying a parade of gilded statues and paintings under a colorfully frescoed ceiling telling stories of Virgin Mary's life. When you reach the altar at the front, turn around and notice how the church suddenly becomes simpler without all that ornamentation. Prague's grandest pipe organ fills the back wall.

As you leave, look for the black, shriveled-up arm with clenched fingers (hanging by a chain from a metal post 15 feet above and to the left of the door). According to legend, a thief attempted to steal the Madonna Pietatis from the altar, but his hand was frozen the moment he touched the statue. The monks had to cut off his arm to get the hand to let go. The desiccated arm now hangs here as a warning.

▶ *Exiting the church, do a U-turn to the left (heading up Jakubská street, along the side of the church, past some rough-looking bars). After one block, turn right on Templová street. Head two blocks down the street (passing a nice view of the Týn Church's rear end, and some deluxe toilets) and go through the arcaded passageway, where you emerge onto...*

⑥ Celetná Street

Since the 10th century, this street has been a corridor in the busy commercial quarter—filled with merchants and guilds. These days, it's still pretty commercial, and very touristy.

Here on Celetná street, you're surrounded by a number of buildings with striking facades. To the left is the medieval Powder Tower—we'll head there soon. Straight ahead of you is a Baroque balcony supported by four statues. Many facades are Neoclassical—pastel colors, with arches over doorways, pediments over windows, and hints of scrollwork and garlands. It's little wonder that, when moviemakers want to film a movie set in frilly Baroque times (such as the movie about Mozart, *Amadeus*), they often choose Prague. In fact, we'll see a historic Mozart-era theater in just a moment.

▶ *To your right is a striking, angular building called the...*

Cubist-inspired House of the Black Madonna

Celetná Street has traditional shops.

❼ House of the Black Madonna (Dům u Černé Matky Boží)

Back around the turn of the 20th century, Prague was a center of avant-garde art second only to Paris. Art Nouveau blossomed here (as we'll soon see), as did Cubism. The Cubist exterior is a marvel of rectangular windows and cornices—stand back and see how masterfully it makes its statement while mixing with its neighbors...then get up close and study the details. The interior houses a Cubist café (the recommended Grand Café Orient, one flight up the parabolic spiral staircase)—complete with cube-shaped chairs and square-shaped rolls. The Kubista gallery on the ground floor shows more examples of this unique style. This building is an example of what has long been considered the greatest virtue of Prague's architects: the ability to adapt grandiose plans to the existing cityscape.

▶ *The long, skinny square that begins just to the left of the House of the Black Madonna is...*

❽ Fruit Market (Ovocný Trh) and the Estates Theater

This long, narrow square with a bulge in the middle is typical of medieval Central European market towns. Market stalls would pop up along the busy main drag right in the center of town—making it easy to see how a town can swell as it grows. While no fruit vendors still sell their wares here, this square has retained its traditional name.

The green-and-white building squatting in the middle of the square—right at the bulge—is the **Estates Theater** (Stavovské Divadlo). Built by a nobleman in the 1780s, this Classicist building was the prime opera venue in Prague at a time when an Austrian prodigy was changing the course of music. Wolfgang Amadeus Mozart premiered *Don Giovanni* in this building (with a bronze statue of Il Commendatore duly flanking the main entrance

Estates Theater—playing Mozart since the 1780s

Powder Tower—once the town's main gate

on the left), and he directed many of his works here. Prague's theatergoers would whistle arias from Mozart's works on the streets the morning after they premiered. Today, the Estates Theater (part of the National Theater group) continues to produce Mozart operas.

▶ *Backtrack a few steps to Celetná street, turn right, and head about 50 yards to the...*

⑨ Powder Tower

The big, black, 500-year-old Powder Tower was the main gate of the old town wall. It also housed the city's gunpowder—hence the name. This is the only surviving bit of the wall that was built to defend the city in the 1400s. (Though you can go inside, it's not worth paying to tour the interior.)

The Powder Tower was the city's formal front door—the road from Vienna entered here. Picture the scene in 1740, when Habsburg Empress Maria Theresa had just been crowned Queen of Bohemia. As she returned home in triumph, she passed through the Powder Tower gate.

Go back 500 years and look up at the impressive Gothic-carved welcoming committee, reminding all of the hierarchy of our mortal existence: Reading from the bottom up, you'll see artisans flanking Prague's coat of arms, a pair of Czech kings with seals of alliance with neighboring regions, angels with golden wings, and saints flanking Christ in majesty. The tower is topped with one of Prague's signature styles—a trapezoidal roof.

▶ *Pass regally through the Powder Tower. In so doing, you're leaving the Old Town. You emerge into a big, busy intersection. To your left is the Municipal House, a cream-colored building topped with a green dome. Find a good spot where you can view the facade.*

⑩ Municipal House (Obecní Dům)

The Municipal House, which celebrated its centennial birthday in 2011, is the "pearl of Czech Art Nouveau." Art Nouveau flourished during the same period as the Eiffel Tower and Europe's great Industrial Age train stations.

The same engineering prowess was harnessed by Art Nouveau architects to create quite the opposite effect: curvy, organically flowing lines, inspired by vines and curvaceous women. Art Nouveau was a reaction against the sterility of modern-age construction. Look at the elaborate wrought-iron balcony—flanked by bronze Atlases hefting their lanterns—and the lovely stained glass (as in the entrance arcade).

Mosaics and sculptural knickknacks (see the faces above the

Prague: The Queen of Art Nouveau

Prague is Europe's best city for Art Nouveau. That's the style of art and architecture that flourished throughout Europe around 1900. It was called "nouveau"—or new—because it was associated with all things modern: technology, social progress, and enlightened thinking. Art Nouveau was neo-nothing, but instead a fresh answer to all the revival styles of the late-19th century, and an organic response to the Eiffel Tower art of the Industrial Age.

By taking advantage of recent advances in engineering, Art Nouveau liberated the artist in each architect. Notice the curves and motifs expressing originality—every facade is unique. Artists such as Alfons Mucha believed that the style should apply to all facets of daily life. They designed everything from buildings and furniture to typefaces and cigarette packs.

Prague's three top Art Nouveau architects are Jan Koula, Josef Fanta, and Osvald Polivka (whose last name sounds like the Czech word for "soup"). Think "Cola, Fanta, and Soup"—easy to remember and a good way to impress your local friends.

Though Art Nouveau was born in Paris, it's in Prague where you'll find some of its greatest hits: the Municipal House and nearby buildings, Grand Hotel Evropa (on Wenceslas Square), the exuberant facades of the Jewish Quarter, the Jerusalem Synagogue, and—especially—the work of Prague's own Alfons Mucha. You can  see his stained-glass window in St. Vitus Cathedral (at Prague Castle), the excellent Mucha Museum (near Wenceslas Square), and his masterpiece, *Slav Epic* (in Veletržní Palace on the city's outskirts).

windows) made the building's facade colorful and joyous. Study the bright mosaic above the balcony, called **Homage to Prague.** A symbol of the city, the goddess Praha presides over a land of peace and high culture—an image that stoked cultural pride and nationalist sentiment. On the balcony is a medallion showing the three-tower castle that is the symbol of Prague.

The Municipal House was built in the early 1900s, when Czech nationalism was at a fever pitch. Having been ruled by the Austrian Habsburgs for the previous 300 years, the Czechs were demanding independence. This building was drenched in patriotic Czech themes. Within a few short years, in 1918, the nation of Czechoslovakia was formed—and the independence proclamation was announced to the people right here, from the balcony of the Municipal House.

The interior of the Municipal House has perhaps Europe's finest Art Nouveau decor. It's free to enter and wander the public areas. Go ahead. (For a description of the interior, see page 124.)

The Municipal House sports Art Nouveau ironwork, murals, and statues, and has a great interior.

▶ *Before moving on, note the building across the street,* **Divaldo Hibernia,** *where concerts are held.*

Now head west down Na Příkopě (to the left as you face the Powder Tower) toward the Metro station about 200 yards away. Enjoy the sights of...

⑪ Na Příkopě, the Old City Wall

The street called Na Příkopě was where the old city wall once stood. More specifically, the name Na Příkopě means "On the Moat," and you're walking along what was once the moat outside the wall. To your right is the Old Town. To the left, the New. Look at your city map and conceptualize medieval Prague's smart design: The city was protected on two sides by its river, and on the other two sides by its walls (marked by the modern streets called Na Příkopě, Revoluční, and Národní Třída). The only river crossing back then was the fortified Charles Bridge.

Though the moat and city wall are now long gone, there's still a strong divide between the Old Town and the New Town. Na Příkopě—with its modern buildings, banks, and workaday franchise stores—is more New than Old. It's bustling and lively, without a hint of the trouble Prague endured in the mid-20th century.

Many of Prague's top shopping malls are along this strip, as well as the **Museum of Communism** (at #10, tucked down a courtyard on your left; see page 122). This homage to the proletariat is nestled, ironically, between a McDonald's and a casino (somewhere, Lenin is rolling over in his grave). For four decades (1945-1989), the Czech people suffered under a communist government, under the thumb of the Soviet Union. Remember, at the end of World War II, it was the Soviet Union that liberated Eastern Europe—including Czechoslovakia—from the Nazis. And they never left.

Pause for a moment—immersed in all of this modern commerce— and ponder the hard times under communism: Prague became a gray and bleak world of decrepit buildings. Consumer goods were scarce— customers waited in line for hours for a tin of pineapple or a bottle of ersatz Coke. Statues were black with soot, and on the Charles Bridge—so busy today—there was nothing but a few shady characters trying to change money. At the train station, frightened but desperate locals would meet arriving foreigners and offer to rent them a room, hoping to earn enough Western cash to buy batteries or Levis at one of the hard-currency stores. Life seemed hopeless. In the spring of 1968, the Czechs tried to rise up,

Learn of Prague's 40 years of oppression.

Wenceslas Square, hub of the New Town

enacting government reforms that came to be called "Prague Spring." But Soviet tanks rumbled into Prague and crushed the rebellion. It wasn't until a generation later, in 1989, that the sad tale finally had its happy ending... and it happened just steps away from here, at our next stop.

▶ *Continue up Na Příkopě street to an intersection (and nearby Metro stop) called Můstek. To your left stretches the vast expanse of the wide boulevard called...*

⑫ Wenceslas Square—the New Town

Wenceslas Square—with the National Museum and landmark statue of St. Wenceslas at the very top—is the centerpiece of Prague's New Town. This square was originally founded as a thriving horse market. Today it's a modern world of high-fashion stores, glitzy shopping malls, fine old facades (and some jarringly modern ones), fast-food restaurants, and sausage stands.

Picture the scene on this square on a cold November night in 1989: The Berlin Wall has fallen, and a student protest in Prague has been put down violently—the last straw for a city that was fed up with the oppressive communist system. Each night for a week and a half, hundreds of thousands of freedom-loving Czechs fill Wenceslas Square, jangling their key chains and demanding their freedom. Finally, the formerly jailed poet/philosopher/dissident Václav Havel appears on a balcony to announce the end of communism. The crowd celebrates wildly, having overthrown the rule of an "Evil Empire" without firing a shot...a feat that has come to be known as the Velvet Revolution. (For more on the Velvet Revolution and Wenceslas Square, see the ✪ Wenceslas Square Walk chapter.)

▶ *Let's plunge back into the Old Town and return to the Old Town Square.*

Turn about face, and head downhill (north) on the street called Na Můstku—"along the bridge" that crossed the moat (příkopě) we've been following until now.

Walk down Na Můstku. After one touristy block, it jogs slightly to the left and becomes Melantrichova. As the many shops of lively Melantrichova street clearly demonstrate, the bleak communist era is already ancient history. Today, Prague bustles, amid an Old World ambience. A block farther along, on the left, is...

⑬ Havelská Market

This open-air market, offering crafts and produce, was first set up in the 13th century for the German trading community. Though heavy on souvenirs these days (especially on weekends), the market still feeds hungry locals and vagabonds cheaply. Lined with inviting benches, it's an ideal place to enjoy a healthy snack—and merchants are happy to sell a single vegetable or piece of fruit. The market is also a fun place to browse for crafts. It's a homegrown, homemade kind of place; you'll often be dealing with the actual artist or farmer. The cafés and little eateries circling the market offer a relaxing vantage point from which to view the action.

▶ *Continue along Melantrichova street. Eventually—after passing increasingly tacky souvenir shops and a "museum of sex machines"—Melantrichova curves right and spills out at the Old Town Square, right by the Astronomical Clock. At the clock, turn left down Karlova street. The rest of our walk follows Karlova (though the road twists and turns a bit) to the Charles Bridge, where our tour ends. Begin by heading along the top of the Small Market Square (Malé Náměstí, with lots of outdoor tables), then follow Karlova's twisting course—Karlova street signs keep you on track, and Karlův Most signs point to the bridge. Or just follow the crowds.*

⑭ Karlova Street

Although traffic-free, Karlova street is utterly jammed with tourists as it winds toward the Charles Bridge. But the route has plenty of historic charm if you're able to ignore the contemporary tourism. As you walk, look up. Notice historic symbols and signs of shops, which advertised who lived there or what they sold. Cornerstones, designed to protect buildings from careening carriages, also date from centuries past.

The touristy feeding-frenzy of today's Prague is at its ugliest along this commercial gauntlet. Obviously, you'll find few good values on this drag. Locals have a disdain for the many Russian-owned shops selling matryoshka nesting dolls, furry hats, and other things that have nothing to do with Czech culture.

Keep walking toward the Charles Bridge. After the street jogs right to cross Husova, many of the buildings you'll see on your right are associated with Prague's **Charles University.** Behind the souvenir stalls lie venerable classrooms and lecture halls. The hidden courtyards have provided Czech scholars with their two most essential needs: a space for spirited conversation and good beer. Imagine Prague in the late 1500s, when it was the center of the Holy Roman Empire, and one of the most enlightened places in Europe. The astronomers Tycho Brahe (who tracked the planets) and his assistant Johannes Kepler (who formulated the laws of motion) both worked here. Charles University has always been at the center of Czech political thinking and revolutions, from Jan Hus in the 15th century to the passionately patriotic Czech students who swept communists out of power in the Velvet Revolution. Today, Charles University still attracts the best and brightest. For Czech students, tuition is free.

The **Klementinum** (which once housed the university's library) is the large building that borders Karlova street on the right. Just past the intersection with Liliová, where the street opens into a little square, turn right through the archway (at #1) and into a tranquil courtyard that feels an eternity away from the touristy hubbub of Karlova. You can also visit the Klementinum's impressive Baroque interior on a guided tour (see page 116).

▸ *Karlova street leads directly to a tall medieval tower that marks the start of the Charles Bridge. But before entering the bridge, stop on this side of the river. To the right of the tower is a little park with a great view of*

Havelská Market—produce, gifts, people

Karlova Street, the (crowded) main drag

both the bridge and the rest of Prague across the river. While it's officially called Křižovnické Náměstí, I think of it as...

⑮ Charles IV Square—The Bohemian Golden Age

Start with the statue of the bridge's namesake, **Charles IV** (1316-1378). Look familiar? He's the guy on the 100-koruna bill. Charles was the Holy Roman Emperor who ruled his vast empire from Prague in the 14th century—a high-water mark in the city's history. The statue shows one of Charles' many accomplishments: He holds a contract establishing Charles University, the first in central Europe. The women around the pedestal symbolize the school's four traditional subjects: theology, the arts, law, and medicine.

Charles was the preeminent figure in Europe in the Late Middle Ages, and the father of the Prague we enjoy today. His domain encompassed the modern Czech Republic and parts of Germany, Austria, and the Low Countries.

Charles was cosmopolitan. Born in Prague, raised in Paris, crowned in Rome, and inspired by the luxury-loving pope in Avignon, Charles returned home bringing Europe's culture with him. Besides founding Charles University, he built the Charles Bridge, Charles Square (where you're standing), much of Prague Castle and St. Vitus Cathedral, and the New Town (modeled on Paris). Charles traded ideas with the Italian poet Petrarch and imported artists from France, Italy, and Flanders (inspiring the art of the Museum of Medieval Art, described on page 118). Under Charles, Prague became the most cultured city in Europe.

Now look up at the **bridge tower** (which you can climb for wonderful views—see page 117). Built by Charles, it's one of the finest Gothic gates anywhere. The statuary shows the 14th-century hierarchy of society: people at street level, above them kings, and bishops above the kings. Speaking of hierarchy, check out Charles' statue from near the street. From this angle, some think the emperor looks like he's peeing on the tourists. Which reminds me, public toilets are nearby.

▶ *Stroll to the riverside, belly up to the bannister, and take in the...*

⑯ View from the River

Before you are the Vltava River and the Charles Bridge. Across the river, atop the hill, is Prague Castle topped by the prickly spires of St. Vitus Cathedral. **Prague Castle** has been the seat of power in this region for

Charles IV made Prague a world capital.

View of the hill-topping castle complex

over a thousand years, since the time of Wenceslas. By some measures, it's the biggest castle on earth. Given the castle's long history, it's no wonder that, when the nation of Czechoslovakia was formed in 1918, Prague Castle served as the "White House" of its new president. If you tour the castle, you also get access to historic St. Vitus Cathedral, which was begun by Emperor Charles IV. The cathedral has the tomb of Wenceslas as well as a stunning Art Nouveau stained-glass window by Alfons Mucha. (For details, ✪ see the Prague Castle Tour chapter.)

The **Vltava River** is better known by its German name, Moldau. It bubbles up from the Šumava Hills in southern Bohemia and runs 270 miles through a diverse landscape, like a thread connecting the Czech people. As we've learned, the Czechs have struggled heroically to carve out their identity while surrounded by mightier neighbors—Austrians, Germans, and Russians. The Vltava is their shared artery.

The **view of the Charles Bridge** from here is photogenic to the max. The historic bridge is almost seven football fields long, lined with lanterns and 30 statues, and bookmarked at each end with medieval towers (both climbable). This structure is not the first that has stood on this spot. In fact, the name "Prague" comes from the word "threshold," because the city was born at a convenient place to cross the wide river and enter a new place. But earlier wooden bridges were washed away by floods. Finally, following a massive flood in 1342, Charles IV commissioned a new stone span—Prague's only bridge for more than 400 years. It connects the Old Town with the district called the Little Quarter at the base of the castle across the river.

▶ *Now wander onto the bridge. Make your way slowly across the bridge, checking out several of the statues, all on the right-hand side.*

⑰ Charles Bridge

Among Prague's defining landmarks, this much-loved bridge offers one of the most pleasant and entertaining strolls in Europe. Musicians, artisans, and a constant parade of people make it a festival every day. You can come back and back to this bridge enjoying its charms differently at various times of day. Early and late, it can be enchantingly lonely. It's a photographer's delight during that "magic hour," when the sun is low in the sky.

The statues on either side of the bridge depict saints, and all of them are impressively expressive. Today, half of these statues are replicas—the originals are in city museums, safe from the polluted air.

Pause at the **third statue** on the right. Originally, there were no statues on the bridge, only a cross. You can still see that cross incorporated into this crucifixion scene. The rest of the bridge's statues were added when the Habsburg Catholics ruled in the 17th and 18th centuries. After the Hussite years, the Habsburgs wanted to make sure the saints overlooked and inspired the townsfolk each day as they crossed what was still the only bridge in town.

Continue two more statues to see **Cyril and Methodius,** the two brothers who brought Christianity to this area around 865. Born in Thessaloniki (part of northern Greece today), Cyril and Methodius are credited with introducing Christianity not only to the Czechs, but to all Slavs; you'll see them revered from here to Dubrovnik, Warsaw, and Vladivostok. In this statue, they're bringing a pagan and primitive (bare-breasted) Czech woman into the Christian fold.

Now continue on, past the next statue, and find a small **brass relief** showing a cross with five stars embedded in the wall of the bridge (it's just below the little grate that sits on top of the stone bannister). The relief

The Charles Bridge spans the Vltava River.

The cross is the Charles Bridge's oldest statue.

depicts a figure floating in the river, with a semicircle of stars above him. This marks the traditional spot where St. John of Nepomuk, the national saint of the Czech people, is believed to have been tossed off the bridge and into the river.

For the rest of that story, continue two more statue groups to the bronze Baroque statue of **St. John of Nepomuk,** with the five golden stars encircling his head. This statue always draws a crowd. John was a 14th-century priest to whom the queen confessed all her sins. According to a 17th-century legend, the king wanted to know his wife's secrets, but Father John dutifully refused to tell. The shiny plaque at the base of the statue shows what happened next: John was tortured and eventually killed by being thrown off the bridge. The plaque shows the heave-ho. When he hit the water, five stars appeared, signifying his purity. Traditionally, people believe that touching the St. John plaque will make a wish come true. But you get only one chance in life to make this wish, so think carefully before you commit.

The Czech people are especially devoted to St. John Nepomuk and a handful of other patron saints who—even if you're an atheist— serve as a rallying point for Czech national identity. Another one, directly across from John, is **St. Ludmila,** who raised her grandson to become St. Wenceslas—the 10th-century duke-turned-saint who first united the Czech people (and whose statue is found at the far end of the bridge).

▶ *A good way to end this walk is to enjoy the city and river view from near the center of the bridge. Stand here and survey your surroundings.*

⓲ View from the Charles Bridge

First, look **upstream.** Notice the icebreakers immediately below. They protect the abutments upon which the bridge sits, as river ice has historically threatened its very survival. Look farther upstream for the tiny locks on the right side. While today's river traffic is limited to tourist boats, in earlier times timber, lashed like rafts, was floated down the river. On the left, farther upstream, by the next bridge, is a building with a gilded crown atop its black dome. That's the National Theater. The rentable paddleboats plying the water (easy and affordable) are a romantic way to get a little exercise (see page 125).

Now, cross over and look **downstream.** Scan from right to left. You'll see the modern Four Seasons Hotel—that's the black roof, doing a pretty good job of fitting in. Farther down (with the green roof), is the large

Neo-Renaissance concert hall of the Czech Philharmonic. Across the river and up the hill is a red needle of a giant metronome (currently stopped). It stands at the spot where a 50-foot-tall granite Joseph Stalin—flanked by eight equally tall deputies—stood from 1955 to 1962. To the right of Stalin's former perch (hiding under the trees and worth the climb on a hot summer day) is Prague's most popular beer garden. Finally, capping the hill, follow the line of noble palaces that leads to the spire of the cathedral. It stands at the center of the castle, which—for a thousand years—has been the political heart of this nation.

And beneath your feet flows the majestic Vltava River, the watery thread that has—and always will—connect the proud Czech people.

▶ *From here, you can continue across the bridge to the Little Quarter (Kampa Island, on your left as you cross the bridge, is a tranquil spot to explore; for more on sights in this area, see page 129). Across the bridge and a 10-minute walk to the right is the Malostranská stop for the Metro or for the handy Tram #22. You can also hike (or ride Tram #22) up to the castle from here. Or retrace your steps across the bridge to enjoy more time in the Old Town.*

Charles Bridge—one of Europe's most atmospheric spots for tourists, buskers, and great views

Jewish Quarter Tour

The fluctuating fortunes of Eastern Europe's Jews are etched in the streets of Prague's historic Jewish Quarter. This three-block area in the Old Town has been home to a Jewish community for a thousand years. The neighborhood features several impressive synagogues (including the oldest medieval one in Europe), an evocative cemetery, a powerful memorial honoring Czech Jews murdered in the Holocaust, and engaging exhibits on Jewish customs and tradition.

For me, this is the most interesting collection of Jewish sights in Europe, and—despite the high admission cost—well worth seeing. All but one of the sights are part of the **Jewish Museum in Prague** (Židovské Muzeum v Praze) and are treated as a single attraction. The remaining sight is the **Old-New Synagogue.**

ORIENTATION

Cost: You have three options: **Ticket #1** ("Jewish Town of Prague")-480 Kč, covers all six Jewish Museum sights plus the Old-New Synagogue; **Ticket #2**-300 Kč, covers Jewish Museum sights only; **Ticket #3**-200 Kč, covers the Old-New Synagogue only. Tickets are good for a week.

You can buy your ticket online (www.jewishmuseum.cz), at the Information Center at Maiselova 15 (near the intersection with Siroka street), or at one of these synagogues: Pinkas, Klausen, or Spanish.

Hours: The six **museum** sights are open April-Oct Sun-Fri 9:00-18:00, Nov-March until 17:00, closed year-round on Sat and Jewish holidays; check the website for a complete list of holiday closures, especially if you are visiting in the fall. The **Old-New Synagogue** is open Sun-Thu 9:30-18:00, Fri until 17:00 or sunset, closed Sat and Jewish holidays (admission includes worthwhile 10-minute tour).

Avoiding Lines: The Pinkas Synagogue can be packed, especially 9:30-12:00, so be there right as it opens or later in the day. To save time in line, buy your ticket in advance at the other less-crowded locations. Also see "Planning Your Time," later.

Dress Code: Men are expected to have their heads covered when entering a synagogue or cemetery. While you'll see many visitors ignoring this custom, it is respectful to borrow a museum-issued yarmulke.

Getting There: The Jewish Quarter is an easy walk from Old Town Square, up delightful Pařížská street (next to the green-domed Church of St. Nicholas). The Staroměstská Metro stop is handy.

Information: Jewish Museum in Prague—tel. 222-317-191, www.jewish museum.cz; Old-New Synagogue—tel. 222-317-191, www.synagogue.cz.

Tours: The museum's **audioguide** (300 Kč, must leave ID) is probably more information than you'll need. Three-hour **group tours** are offered by Wittmann Tours. Tours meet in the little park (just beyond the café), directly in front of Hotel InterContinental at the end of Pařížská street (880-Kč—which includes admissions, May-Oct Sun-Fri at 10:30 and 14:00, Nov-Dec and mid-March-April Sun-Fri at 10:30 only, no tours Sat and Jan-mid-March, tel. 603-168-427 or 603-426-564, www.wittmann-tours.com). Also, many **private guides** do good tours of the Jewish Quarter (see page 180).

Maisel Synagogue, with its excellent museum, is a good introduction to the Jewish Quarter.

Length of This Tour: Allow three hours (which could be split over several days—your ticket is good for a week). With limited time, focus on the Old-New Synagogue (for the ambience); the Pinkas Synagogue and Old Jewish Cemetery (for the history); and the Maisel Synagogue (for its exhibits).

Photos: While *No Photo* signs are posted everywhere, photos without flash seem to be allowed (except during prayer times at the Old-New Synagogue). Photography is permitted in the cemetery if you pay a 40-Kč fee.

Services: A café and WCs are at the ticket office at Maiselova 15.

Starring: The synagogues and cemetery of a faith and culture that has left its mark on Prague.

Planning Your Time

Your ticket comes with a map that locates the sights and lists admission appointments—the times you'll be let in if it's very busy. (Ignore the times unless it's extremely crowded.) You'll notice plenty of security, which can slow down entry.

You can see the sights in any order. This plan works well: Buy your ticket at the Information Center. Visit the Maisel Synagogue for its museum-quality exhibits, which provide a good introduction. Next is the Jewish Quarter's most popular (and crowded) sight, the Pinkas Synagogue, a sobering reminder of Holocaust victims. This leads into the Old Jewish Cemetery, crowded with tombstones. The small Ceremonial Hall covers burial rites, and the Klausen Synagogue has more informative exhibits. Break for coffee, then visit the Old-New Synagogue to soak up its majestic, medieval ambience. Finish with the ornately decorated Spanish Synagogue and its fine exhibits that bring Jewish history up to the moment.

Alternatively, you could plan your time around the crowded Pinkas Synagogue. Ideally, to avoid the crowds, be there right as it opens or visit late in the day.

Background

The Jewish people from the Holy Land (today's Israel and Palestine) were dispersed by the Romans nearly 2,000 years ago. Over the centuries, their culture survived in enclaves throughout the world; it was said that "the Torah was their sanctuary, which no army could destroy."

Jews first came to Prague in the 10th century. The least habitable, marshy area closest to the bend was allotted to the Jewish community. The Jewish Quarter's main intersection (Maiselova and Široká streets) was the meeting point of two medieval trade routes. For centuries, Jews coexisted—at times tensely—with their non-Jewish Czech neighbors.

During the Crusades in the 12th century, the pope declared that Jews and Christians should not live together. Jews had to wear yellow badges, and their quarter was walled in and became a ghetto (minority neighborhood) of wooden houses and narrow lanes. In the 16th and 17th centuries, Prague had one of the biggest ghettos in Europe, with 11,000 inhabitants. Within its six gates, Prague's Jewish Quarter was a gaggle of 200 wooden buildings.

Faced with institutionalized bigotry and harassment, Jews relied mainly on profits from moneylending (forbidden to Christians) and community solidarity to survive. While their money bought them protection (the kings taxed Jewish communities heavily), it was often also a curse. Throughout Europe, when times got tough and Christian debts to the Jewish community mounted, entire Jewish communities were evicted or

The former Jewish ghetto now sports some of the city's toniest Art Nouveau facades.

The Synagogue

A synagogue is a place of public worship, where Jews gather to pray, sing, and read from the Torah. Most synagogues have similar features, though they vary depending on the congregation.

The synagogue generally faces toward Jerusalem (so in Prague, worshippers face east). At the east end is an alcove called the **ark,** which holds the Torah. These scriptures (the first five books of the Old Testament) are written in Hebrew on scrolls wrapped in luxuriant cloth. The other main element of the synagogue is the **bema,** a platform from which the Torah is read aloud. In traditional Orthodox synagogues (like some in the Jewish Quarter), the bema is near the center of the hall, and the reader stands facing the same direction as

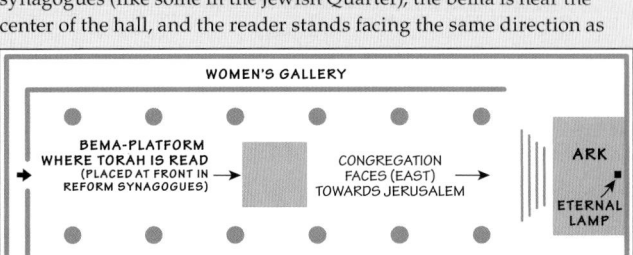

killed. In the Prague pogrom of 1389, a Christian mob massacred inhabitants of the Jewish quarter and set it ablaze.

In 1781, Emperor Josef II, motivated more by economic concerns than by religious freedom, eased much of the discrimination against Jews. In 1848, the Jewish Quarter's walls were torn down, and the neighborhood—named Josefov in honor of the emperor who provided this small measure of tolerance—was incorporated as a district of the Old Town.

In 1897, ramshackle Josefov was razed and replaced by a new modern town—the original 31 streets and 220 buildings became 10 streets and 83 buildings. They leveled the medieval-era buildings (except the synagogues) and turned this into perhaps Europe's finest Art Nouveau neighborhood. All along this walk you'll enjoy stately facades with gables, the congregation. (In other branches of Judaism, the bema is at the front, and the reader faces the worshippers.) Orthodox synagogues have separate worship areas for men and women, usually with women in the balcony.

The synagogue walls might be decorated with elaborate patterns of vines or geometric designs, but never statues of people, as that might be seen as idol worship. A lamp above the ark is always kept lit, as it was in the ancient temple of Jerusalem, and candelabras called menorahs also recall the temple. Other common symbols are the two tablets of the Ten Commandments given to Moses or a Star of David, representing the Jewish king's shield.

At a typical service, the congregation arrives at the start of Sabbath (Friday evening). As a sign of respect toward God, men don yarmulkes (small round caps). As the cantor leads songs and prayers, worshippers follow along in a book of weekly readings. At the heart of the service, everyone stands as the Torah is ceremoniously paraded, unwrapped, and placed on the bema. Someone—the rabbi, the cantor, or a congregant—reads the words aloud. The rabbi ("teacher") might give a commentary on the Torah passage.

Services similar to this have gone on in Prague's Jewish Quarter for a thousand years.

turrets, elegant balconies, mosaics, statues, and all manner of architectural marvels. By the 1930s, Prague's Jewish community was prospering.

But then World War II hit. Of the 55,000 Jews living in Prague in 1939, just 10,000 survived the Holocaust to see liberation in 1945. And in the communist era—when the atheistic regime was also anti-Semitic—recovery was slow.

Today there are only 3,000 "registered" Jews in the Czech Republic, and of these, only 1,700 are in Prague. (There are probably more Jewish people here, but after their experiences with the Nazis and communists, it's understandable that many choose not to register.) Today, in spite of their tiny numbers, the legacy of Prague's Jewish community lives on. While today's modern grid plan has replaced the higgledy-piggledy medieval streets of old, Široká ("Wide Street") remains the main street. A few Jewish-themed shops and restaurants in the area add extra ambience to this (otherwise modern) neighborhood.

THE TOUR BEGINS

▶ *Start at the center of the neighborhood, the intersection of Maiselova and Široká streets. A half-block south on Maiselova street is the...*

❶ Maisel Synagogue (Maiselova Synagóga)

Before entering, notice the facade featuring the Ten Commandments top and center (standard in synagogues). Below that is the symbol for Prague's Jewish community: the Star of David, with the pointed hat local Jews wore here through medieval times.

This synagogue was built as a private place of worship for the Maisel family during the late 16th century. This was a "Golden Age" for Prague's Jews, when Habsburg rulers lifted the many bans and persecutions against them. Maisel, the wealthy financier of the Habsburg king, lavished his riches on the synagogue's Neo-Gothic interior.

In World War II, the synagogue became a warehouse for Jewish artifacts. The Nazis had ordered Jewish synagogues all over the Czech world to send their riches to Prague—Torah scrolls, books, menorahs—to be part of a Jewish museum. Some think that Hitler had a more diabolical plan: to eliminate the Jews altogether, then preserve their artifacts in what was to be a "Museum of the Extinct Jewish Race."

Pinkas Synagogue lists Holocaust victims.

Displays about Jewish culture

Prague's Jewish Quarter

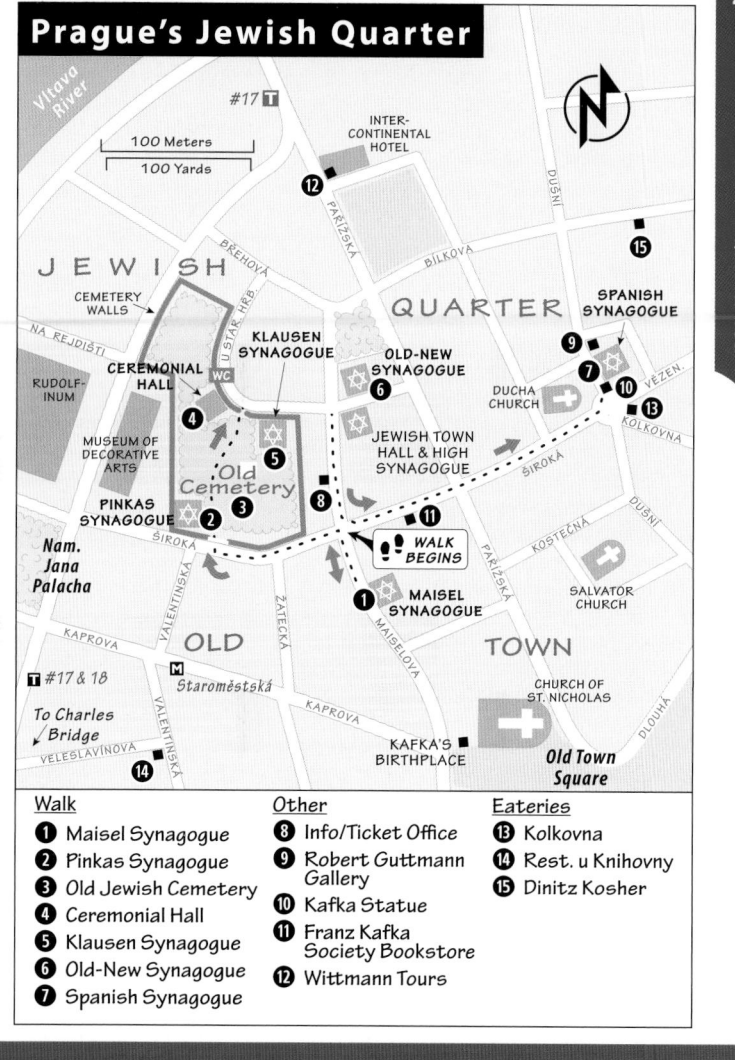

Vltava River

#17 🚊

INTER-CONTINENTAL HOTEL

100 Meters
100 Yards

⑫ Wittmann Tours

PAŘÍŽSKÁ

DUŠNÍ

⑮

BŘEHOVÁ

BÍLKOVÁ

J E W I S H

QUARTER

SPANISH SYNAGOGUE

CEMETERY WALLS

NA REJDIŠTI

U STAR. HŘB.

KLAUSEN SYNAGOGUE

OLD-NEW SYNAGOGUE
⑥

⑨
⑦

VĚZEŇ

CEREMONIAL HALL

WC

DUCHA CHURCH

⑩

RUDOLF-INUM

KOLKOVNÁ

⑬

MUSEUM OF DECORATIVE ARTS

④

⑤

JEWISH TOWN HALL & HIGH SYNAGOGUE

ŠIROKÁ

DUŠNÍ

Old Cemetery

③

⑧

②

PINKAS SYNAGOGUE

Nam. Jana Palacha

ŠIROKÁ

ŽATECKÁ

WALK BEGINS

⑪

KOSTEČNÁ

PAŘÍŽSKÁ

SALVATOR CHURCH

①

MAISEL SYNAGOGUE

KAPROVA

M

VALENTINSKÁ

Staroměstská

MAISELOVA

OLD

TOWN

CHURCH OF ST. NICHOLAS

🚊 #17 & 18

To Charles Bridge

KAPROVA

DLOUHÁ

VELESLAVÍNOVA

VALENTINSKÁ

⑭

KAFKA'S BIRTHPLACE

Old Town Square

Walk
1. Maisel Synagogue
2. Pinkas Synagogue
3. Old Jewish Cemetery
4. Ceremonial Hall
5. Klausen Synagogue
6. Old-New Synagogue
7. Spanish Synagogue

Other
8. Info/Ticket Office
9. Robert Guttmann Gallery
10. Kafka Statue
11. Franz Kafka Society Bookstore
12. Wittmann Tours

Eateries
13. Kolkovna
14. Rest. u Knihovny
15. Dinitz Kosher

Inside, the exhibit—well-explained in English—shows nearly a thousand years of Jewish history in Bohemia and Moravia, told through the use of displays, artifacts, and touch screens (allowing you to view Hebrew maps and manuscripts). Exhibits along the walls cover the status of Jews during medieval times, their golden age (during the Renaissance), their day-to-day lives, discrimination, oppression, and Jewish enlightenment. An audio-visual virtual tour, projected on a screen, "flies" over the Jewish Quarter.

The synagogue hosts concerts and recitals on some evenings.

▸ *Return to Široká street and turn left—following the cemetery wall—to find the...*

❷ Pinkas Synagogue (Pinkasova Synagóga)

A site of Jewish worship since the 16th century, this synagogue is certainly historic. But these days it's best known as a poignant memorial to the victims of the Nazis.

Enter and go down the steps leading to the **main hall** of this small Gothic synagogue. Aaron Meshulam Horowitz, a prosperous merchant and man of influence in his day, built the synagogue in 1535. Notice the old stone-and-wrought-iron bema in the middle, the niche for the ark at the far end, the crisscross vaulting overhead, and the Art Nouveau stained glass filling the place with light.

But the main focus of this synagogue is its walls, inscribed with the handwritten **names** of 77,297 Czech Jews sent to the gas chambers at Auschwitz and other camps. Czech Jews were especially hard hit by the Holocaust. More than 155,000 of them passed through the nearby Terezín camp alone. Most died with no grave marker, but they are remembered here.

The names are carefully organized: Family names are in red, followed in black by the individual's first name, birthday, and date of death (if known) or date of deportation. You can tell by the dates that families often perished together.

The names are gathered in groups by hometowns (listed in gold, as well as on placards at the base of the wall). Prague's dead fill the main hall. On the ark wall is a list of the ghettos and extermination camps that received Czech Jews—Terezín, as well as Dachau, Bergen-Belsen, and the notorious Oświęcim (Auschwitz). As you ponder this sad sight, you'll hear the somber reading of the names alternating with a cantor singing the Psalms.

The Pinkas Synagogue's Gothic main hall has the *bema*—the platform from which the Torah is read.

Among the names are the grandparents of (Prague-born) former US Secretary of State Madeleine Albright—Arnost and Olga Korbel, listed at the far end of the long wall.

Climb eight steps into the **women's gallery,** where (as is typical in traditional synagogues) the women worshipped separately from the men. On the left wall, upper part, find some names in poor condition. These are some of the oldest. You see, the name project began in the 1950s. But the communist regime closed the synagogue and erased virtually everything. With freedom, in 1989, the Pinkas Synagogue was reopened and the names had to be rewritten. These are originals.

On your way out, watch on the right for the easy-to-miss stairs up to the small **Terezín Children's Art Exhibit.** Well-described in English, these drawings were made by Jewish children imprisoned at Terezín, 40 miles northwest of Prague. This is where the Nazis shipped Prague's Jews for processing before transporting them east to death camps. Thirty-five thousand Jews died at Terezín, and many tens of thousands more died in other camps.

Of the 8,000 children transported from Terezín, only 240 survived until liberation. Their art looks like something from your typical elementary school—until you recall the tragic circumstances in which it was created. The collection is organized into poignant themes: dreams of returning to Prague; yearning for a fantasized Holy Land; sentimental memories of the simple times before imprisonment; biblical and folkloric tales focusing on the themes of good and evil; and scenes of everyday life at Terezín. Perhaps saddest of all are the photographs of a few of these young artists. (Terezín makes an emotionally moving day trip from Prague.)

▶ *Exiting the Pinkas Synagogue, the visit leads up several stairs into the adjoining cemetery.*

❸ Old Jewish Cemetery (Starý Židovský Hřbitov)

You enter one of the most wistful scenes in Europe—Prague's Old Jewish Cemetery. You meander along a path through 12,000 evocative tombstones. They're old, eroded, inscribed in Hebrew, and leaning this way and that. A few of the dead have larger ark-shaped tombs. Most have a simple epitaph with the name, date, and a few of the deceased's virtues. Among the dead buried here are Aaron Meshulam Horowitz (builder of the Pinkas Synagogue), Mordecai Maisel (of the Maisel Synagogue), and Rabbi Loew (of golem fame; see "From Golems to Robots" sidebar).

From 1439 until 1787, this was the only burial ground allowed for the Jews of Prague. Over time, the graves had to be piled on top of each other—layered seven or eight deep—so there are actually closer to 85,000 dead here. Graves were never relocated because of the Jewish belief that, once buried, a body should not be moved. Layer by layer, the cemetery grew into a small plateau. And as things settled over time, the tombstones became crooked. Tune into the noise of passing cars outside, and you realize that you're several feet above the modern street level—which is already high above the medieval level.

People place pebbles on honored tombstones. This custom, a sign of respect, shows that the dead have not been forgotten and recalls the old days, when rocks were placed upon a sandy gravesite to keep the body covered. Others leave scraps of paper that contain prayers and wishes. The most popular tombstone on which to place pebbles, coins, and paper is the reddish tomb found alongside the wall (the path leads right by it). This is the burial site of Prague's beloved Rabbi Loew. The cemetery is called Beth Chaim in Hebrew, meaning "House of Life."

▶ *The cemetery visit spills out at the far end, right at the entrances to the Ceremonial Hall (on your left) and Klausen Synagogue (right).*

The Old Jewish Cemetery, once the only place Prague's Jews could be buried, is full of tombstones.

❹ Ceremonial Hall (Obřadní Síň)

This rustic stone tower (1911) was a mortuary house used to prepare the body and perform purification rituals before burial. The inside is painted in fanciful, flowery Neo-Romanesque style. It's filled with a worthwhile exhibition on Jewish medicine, death, and burial traditions. A series of crude but instructive paintings (c. 1780, hanging on walls throughout the house) show how the "burial brotherhood" took care of the ill and buried the dead. As all are equal before God, the rich and poor alike were buried in embroidered linen shrouds similar to the one you'll see on display.

▶ *Next door is the...*

❺ Klausen Synagogue (Klauzová Synagóga)

The 17th-century Baroque-style synagogue is impressive and historic—again, locate the bema, the ark, and the women's gallery above—but the focus here is the displays on Jewish religious practices.

Ground-floor displays touch on Jewish holidays. The bema displays a Torah (the first five books of the Old Testament) and the solid silver pointers used when reading it—necessary since the Torah is not to be touched. Now start at the entrance and work clockwise. In the first big, horizontal display case, the biggest book is a Torah (1444) associated with the great medieval philosopher Maimonides. The second display case has shofar horns, blown ritually during Jewish high holy days. Up in the elevated area, the ark contains elaborately wrapped Torah scrolls ornamented with silver. In the next cases you'll see a seder plate, used to serve the six traditional foods of Passover; a tiny "Omer Calendar," an ingenious device used to keep track of the holidays; and a palm frond *(lulav)*, waved when reciting a blessing during the holiday of Sukkot. At the back of the synagogue are objects from the Prague community, including menorahs used in both synagogues and the Hanukkah celebration.

Upstairs, exhibits illustrate the rituals of everyday Jewish life. It starts at birth. There are good-luck amulets to ensure a healthy baby, and a wooden cradle that announces, "This little one will become big." The male baby is circumcised (see the knife) and grows to celebrate a coming-of-age Bar Mitzvah—girls celebrate a Bat Mitzvah—around age 12 or 13. Marriage takes place under a canopy, and the couple set up their home—the exhibit ends with some typical furnishings.

▶ *Exiting the synagogue, turn right and go one block down to the...*

Klausen Synagogue, with its women's gallery (left), ark for Torah scrolls (far end), and displays

⑥ Old-New Synagogue (Staronová Synagóga, a.k.a. Altneuschul)

For more than 700 years, this has been the most important synagogue and the central building in Josefov. Built in 1270, it's the oldest synagogue in Eastern Europe (and some say the oldest still-working synagogue in all of Europe). The name likely reflects that it was "New" when built, but became "Old" when other, newer synagogues came on the scene. The exterior is simple, with a unique saw-tooth gable. Standing like a bomb-hardened bunker, it feels as though it has survived plenty of hard times.

As you enter, you descend a few steps below street level to 13th-century street level and the medieval world.

The **interior** is pure Gothic—thick pillars, soaring arches, and narrow lancet windows. If it looks like a church, well, the architects were Christians. The stonework is original, and the woodwork (the paneling and benches) is also old. This was one of the first Gothic buildings in Prague.

Seven centuries later, it's still a working synagogue. There's the stone bema in the middle where the Torah is read aloud, and the ark at the far end, where the sacred scrolls are kept. To the right of the ark, one chair is bigger, with a Star of David above it. This chair always remains empty out of respect for great rabbis of the past. Where's the women's gallery? Here, women worshipped in rooms that flanked the hall, watching the service through those horizontal windows in the walls.

The big red banner rising above the bema is (a copy of) a gift from Charles IV, given in honor of the Jewish community's service to the crown. For centuries it has been proudly carried by the Jewish community during parades. On the banner is a Star of David and the Hebrew prayer at the heart of the service: "Hear, O Israel..." Within the Star of David is pictured the yellow-pointed hat that Jewish men were obliged to wear.

The Old-New Synagogue may be Europe's oldest.

Its interior still looks medieval.

From Golems to Robots

One of Judaism's most popular legends is associated with the Old-New Synagogue. Around 1600, Rabbi Loew (who was indeed a real person) wanted to protect Prague's Jews from persecution. So he created a creature out of Vltava River clay, known as the golem. He placed a stone called the *šém* ("word" in Hebrew) in the golem's forehead (or, some say, under his tongue), bringing the beast to life.

The golem guarded the ghetto, but—in keeping with the Jewish custom of reserving the Sabbath as the day of rest—Rabbi Loew always removed the *šém* on Friday night. But one day he forgot, the golem went on a rampage, and Rabbi Loew had to remove the *šém* for good. He hid the golem in the attic of the Old-New Synagogue, where it's said to be to this day. The attic is closed to tourists, but you can circle around behind the building to see an iron-rung ladder that leads to the still-dangerous lair of the golem. Meanwhile, believers in such legends remain convinced that the *šém* can still be found somewhere in the streets of Prague—keep an eye out.

The story of the golem inspired the early 20th-century Czech writer Karel Čapek to write his play *R.U.R.*, about artificially created beings who eventually turn on their creators. To describe the creatures, he coined the Czech word *roboti*, "workers"— which was quickly absorbed into English as "robot."

Twelve is a popular number in the decor, because it symbolizes the 12 tribes of Israel: There are 12 windows, 12 vines in the frieze at the base of the bema, 12 bunches of grapes carved over the entrance, and so on. While Nazis routinely destroyed synagogues, this most historic synagogue in the country survived because the Nazis intended it to be part of their "Museum of the Extinct Jewish Race."

Notice that the ceiling has clumsy five-ribbed vaulting. The builders were good at four-ribbed vaulting, but it wasn't right for a synagogue, because it resulted in a cross.

▶ *The Spanish Synagogue is four blocks from here. Before moving on, check out the building next door (where they sell the tickets for the Old-New Synagogue). This is where Prague's Jews were rounded up before being shipped off to Terezín.*

To reach the Spanish Synagogue, head up Maiselova street (toward Old Town Square), and turn left on Široká, which leads to the...

❼ Spanish Synagogue (Španělská Synagóga)

In its size and ornateness, this building is typical of many synagogues built around Central Europe in the late 1800s. With the formation of the Austro-Hungarian Empire in 1867, Jews were finally granted full rights. Many Jews prospered, as evidenced by this beautiful synagogue.

Before entering, circle around the left side of the building for a better view of the facade. It's called "Spanish" but the style is really Moorish: horseshoe arches atop slender columns, different colored stone, elaborate tracery, and topped with pseudo-minarets. Though the building is relatively new, it stands on the site of Prague's oldest synagogue (from c. 1150), which burned down during the horrific pogrom of 1389.

Inside, the decor is exotic and awe-inspiring. Intricate interweaving designs (of stars and vines) cover every inch of the red-gold and green walls and ceiling. A rose window with a stylized Star of David graces the ark.

The new synagogue housed a new movement within Judaism—a Reform congregation—which worshipped in a more modern way. The bema has been moved to the front of the synagogue, so the reader of the

The Spanish Synagogue, in Moorish style

Its interior walls have elaborate designs.

Torah faces the congregation. There's also a prominent organ (upper right) to accompany the singing.

Displays of Jewish history bring us through the 18th, 19th, and tumultuous 20th centuries to today. In the 1800s, Jews were increasingly accepted and successful in the greater society. But tolerance brought a dilemma—was it better to assimilate within the dominant culture or to join the growing Zionist homeland movement? To reform the religion or to remain orthodox?

Upstairs, the **balcony exhibits** focus on the 1900s. Start in the area near the organ, which explains the late 19th-century development of Josefov. Then work your way around the balcony, with exhibits on Jewish writers (Franz Kafka), philosophers (Edmund Husserl), and other notables (Freud). This intellectual renaissance came to an abrupt halt with World War II and the mass deportations to Terezín (see more sad displays on life there, including more children's art and a box full of tefillin prayer cases). The final displays bring it home: After 2,000 years of living away from their Holy Land roots, the Jewish people had a homeland—the modern nation of Israel.

Finish your visit across the landing in the **Winter Synagogue,** showing a trove of silver—Kiddush cups, Hanukkah lamps, Sabbath candlesticks, and Torah ornaments. This collection got its start in the early 20th century, when the Jewish Museum was formed—and began its important work of preserving places and artifacts that otherwise might have been forever lost.

▶ *Our walk is over. Next door to the Spanish Synagogue is the Robert Guttmann Gallery of temporary exhibits, which is included in your combo-ticket.*

Next to the Spanish Synagogue is a fun, bizarre, photo-op-friendly statue meant to (somehow) depict the writer **Franz Kafka.** *Kafka was a Jew who lived most of his life near here. Fans can find a plaque on the wall at the place he was born (at the corner of Maiselova and the aptly named Náměstí Franze Kafky, a block south of the Maisel Synagogue, near the Church of St. Nicholas).*

Wenceslas Square Walk

Though the Old Town gets all the attention (and all the tourists), the New Town—and particularly its main square—is more the people's Prague. In the 14th century, the king created this new town, tripling the size of what would become Prague. This short walk focuses on the New Town's center-piece, Wenceslas Square—once the horse market of this busy working-class district. Along the way, we'll see sights associated with the square's great moments in history, including the watershed protests of 1989 that helped create the modern nation.

ORIENTATION

Length of This Walk: Allow an hour.

When to Go: As this walk doesn't focus on sights with limited hours, it can be done at any time—and may work particularly well in the evening, after other sights have closed.

Getting There: The walk starts at the very top of Wenceslas Square, in front of the National Museum; the nearest Metro stop is called Muzeum. If you're coming from the Old Town, it's probably easiest just to hike the length of the square up to the top to start the walk.

Eating: This walk passes a popular ice-cream parlor, and dozens of other eateries are nearby; for the best choices, see my recommendations on page 150.

Starring: Urban bustle, a secluded garden, and a thousand years of Czech history—from St. Václav to Václav Havel.

THE WALK BEGINS

▶ *At the top of Wenceslas Square, stand under the huge statue of "Good King Wenceslas" on a horse.*

Wenceslas Square

Join Wenceslas as he gazes proudly down this long, broad square. It's actually more like a boulevard busy with cars, with a park-like median right down the middle. It's a huge expanse, covering more than 10 acres. Stand here, and take in the essence of modern Prague.

Think of how this place has served as a kind of national stage for important events in the history of the Czech people. In 1918, it was here that jubilant crowds gathered to celebrate the end of World War I and the subsequent creation of modern Czechoslovakia. During World War II, this was the scene of Nazi occupation, and then of rioting Czechs who drove the Nazis out. In the spring of 1968, the Czechs gathered here to protest against their next set of oppressors, the communist Soviets. These "Prague Spring" reforms gained international attention, but eventually Soviet tanks rumbled into town and crushed the rebellion. Then in 1989, more than 300,000 Czechs and Slovaks converged right here to reclaim their freedom once again.

View down Wenceslas Square, covering 10 acres

Wenceslas Square, for both cars and people

Which brings us to today. Survey the square for a snapshot of "the now." You'll see businesspeople, families, Dumpster divers, security guards, hipsters, and students. It sums up the changes and rapid transformation of society here over the past 100 years.

▶ *But let's go back to the very beginning. Turn your attention now to the big equestrian statue of...*

❶ Duke Wenceslas I

The "Good King" of Christmas-carol fame was actually a wise and benevolent 10th-century duke. Václav I (as he's called by locals) united the Czech people, back when this land was known as Bohemia. A rare example of a well-educated and literate ruler, Wenceslas Christianized and lifted the culture. He astutely allied the powerless Czechs with the Holy Roman Empire. And he began to fortify Prague's castle as a center of Czech government. After his murder in 929, Wenceslas was canonized as a saint. He became a symbol of Czech nationalism (and appears on the 20-Kč coin). Later kings knelt before his tomb to be crowned. And he remains an icon of Czech unity whenever the nation has to rally. Like King Arthur in England, Wenceslas is more legend than history, but he symbolizes the country's birth.

Legend has it that when the Czechs face their darkest hour, Wenceslas will come riding out of Blaník Mountain (east of Prague) to save them. For centuries, superstitious Czechs have gone to Blaník Mountain at critical points in their history, only to be disappointed. Cynical Czechs today say, "If Wenceslas hasn't come out yet, the worst times must still lie ahead..."

The statue is surrounded by the four other Czech patron saints.

Wenceslas Square Walk

WALK ENDS

WALK BEGINS

250 Meters

250 Yards

1. Duke Wenceslas I Statue
2. National Museum
3. Communist-Era Building
4. Memorial to the Victims of 1969
5. Walking down Wenceslas Square
6. Grand Hotel Evropa
7. The Velvet Revolution
8. Lucerna Arcade
9. Světozor Mall
10. Franciscan Garden
11. Jungmann Square
12. Baťa Shoe Store
13. Můstek & Old City Wall

Notice the focus on books. A small nation without great military power, the Czechs have thinkers as national heroes, not warriors.

And this statue is a popular meeting point. Locals like to say, "I'll meet you under the horse's tail" (though they use a cruder term).

▶ *Circle behind the statue and stand below that tail, and turn your attention to the impressive building at the top of Wenceslas Square.*

❷ National Museum

The building is grand and the interior is rich, though the collection itself is dull. The building dates from the 19th century, back when there was no unified Czech nation—just Czech-speaking peasants living under Austrian Habsburg rule. This bold Neo-Renaissance building was a way to show the world that the Czech people had a distinct culture, a heritage of precious artifacts, and that they deserved their own nation.

Look closely at the columns on the building's facade. Those light-colored patches are covering holes where Soviet bullets hit during the 1968 crackdown. The repair masons did an intentionally sloppy job, so that dark moment could never be plastered over and forgotten.

▶ *To the left of the National Museum (as you face it) is a...*

❸ Communist-Era Building

This ugly, modern structure once housed the rubber-stamp Czechoslovak Parliament back when it voted in lock-step with Moscow. At its base, under the canopy, is a statue from those days, in the style known as Socialist Realism. As was typical, it shows not just a worker...but a triumphant worker.

In addition to this building, the communist authorities also built the nearby Muzeum Metro stop and the busy highway that runs in front of the

National Museum—symbol of 19th-century nationalism

A blocky symbol of 20th-century communism

National Museum. Fortunately, Soviet buildings like this one are quite rare in Prague. Because there was almost no WWII bombing in the city center, the communists had little opportunity to rebuild.

Since the communists checked out, city leaders have struggled with the legacy of this heavy-handed Soviet infrastructure. Between 1994 and 2008, this particular building was home to Radio Free Europe. The grateful Czechs had rented the office space to RFE for 1 Kč a year, as thanks for keeping them in touch with real news during the communist occupation.

▶ *Start walking down Wenceslas Square. Pause about 30 yards along, at the little patch of bushes. In the ground on the downhill side of those bushes is a...*

❹ Memorial to the Victims of 1969

After the Russian crackdown of 1968, a group of patriots wanted to stand up to the powerful Soviet occupation. One was a young philosophy student named Jan Palach. He decided that the best way to stoke the flame of independence was to set himself on fire. On January 16, 1969, Palach stood on the steps of the National Museum and ignited his body for the cause of Czech freedom. He died a few days later in a hospital ward. A month later, another student did the same thing, followed by another. Czechs are keen on anniversaries, and—20 years after Palach's brave and patriotic act, in 1989—Czechs gathered here for a huge demonstration. A sense of new possibility swept through the city, and 10 months later, the communists were history.

▶ *Continue down Wenceslas Square. Our next stop is the median in front of Grand Hotel Evropa. It's the ornate, yellow building about 300 yards down Wenceslas Square, on the right.*

❺ Walking down Wenceslas Square—the New Town

Wenceslas Square is part of Prague's New Town, one of the four traditional quarters. Prague got its start in the ninth century at the castle. It spilled across the river to the Old Town, which was fortified with a city wall. By the 1300s, the Old Town was bursting at the seams. King Charles IV expanded the town outward, tripling the size of Prague. Wenceslas Square, a central feature of the New Town, was originally founded as a horse market.

As you continue walking, notice the architecture, a showcase of architectural styles from the past two centuries: You'll see Neo-Gothic, Neo-Renaissance, and Neo-Baroque from the 19th century. There's

Plaque honoring martyrs for freedom

One of Europe's best Art Nouveau facades

curvaceous Art Nouveau from around 1900. And there's the modernist response to Art Nouveau—Functionalism from the mid-20th century, where the watchword was "form follows function" and beauty took a back seat to practicality. You'll see what's nicknamed "Stalin Gothic" from the 1950s communist era; a good example of that is the Hotel Jalta building, halfway downhill on the right (the sandy facade with lots of balconies). And there are forgettable glass-and-steel buildings of the 1970s.

On the right-hand side of Wenceslas Square is ⑥ **Grand Hotel Evropa.** It's the one with the dazzling yellow Art Nouveau exterior and plush café interior full of tourists. Take a peek inside.

Opposite Grand Hotel Evropa (that is, on the left side of the square), find the Marks & Spencer building, which has a **balcony** on it (partly obscured by tree branches).

▶ *Standing here in the center of Wenceslas Square, look up at that balcony and take a moment to consider the events of November 1989.*

⑦ The Velvet Revolution

Picture the scene on this square on a cold night: November 17, 1989. Czechoslovakia had been oppressed for the previous 40 years by communist Russia. But now the Soviet empire was beginning to crumble, jubilant Germans were dancing on top of the shattered Berlin Wall, and the Czechs were getting a whiff of freedom.

Czechoslovakia's revolution began with a bunch of teenagers, who—following a sanctioned gathering—decided to march on Wenceslas Square. After they were surrounded and beaten by the communist riot police, their enraged parents, friends, and other members of the community began to pour into this square to protest. Night after night, this huge square was filled with more than 300,000 ecstatic Czechs and Slovaks who believed freedom was at hand. Each night they would jangle their key chains in the air as if saying to their communist leaders, "It's time for you to go home now." Finally they gathered and found that their communist overlords had left—and freedom was theirs.

On that night, as thousands filled this square, a host of famous people appeared on that balcony to greet the crowd. There was a well-known priest and a rock star famous for his rebellion against authority. There was Alexander Dubček, the hero of the Prague Spring reforms of 1968. And there was Václav Havel, the charismatic playwright who had spent years in prison, becoming a symbol of resistance—a kind of Czech Nelson Mandela. Now he was free. Havel's voice boomed over the gathered masses. He proclaimed the resignation of the Politburo and the imminent freedom of the Republic of Czechoslovakia. He pulled out a ring of keys and jingled it. Thousands of keys jingled back in response. It was their symbolic way of saying: the communists have packed up and left, and now we're free to unlock our chains.

In previous years, the communist authorities would have sent in tanks to crush the impudent masses. But by 1989, the Soviet empire was collapsing, and the Czech government was shaky. Locals think that Soviet head of state Mikhail Gorbachev (mindful of the Tiananmen Square massacre a few months before) might have made a phone call recommending a nonviolent response. Whatever happened, the communist regime was overthrown with hardly any blood being spilled. It was done through sheer people power—thanks largely to the masses of defiant Czechs who gathered here peacefully in Wenceslas Square. They called it "The Velvet Revolution."

▶ *Look downhill to the bottom of Wenceslas Square. We'll be heading there eventually. But we'll take a less-touristed detour to the left, with some interesting things to see.*

Opposite Grand Hotel Evropa is a shopping mall called the Lucerna Arcade. Use the entry marked Pasáž Rokoko *and walk straight in. Continue about 100 yards straight through the mall until you find a horse hanging from the ceiling.*

❽ Lucerna Arcade

This grand mall retains some of its Art Deco glamour from the 1930s. But that's not its most notable feature. In the middle of it all, you'll see a

A modern artist's take on King Wenceslas; it's in the Lucerna Mall, a great place to just hang.

sculpture—called **Wenceslas Riding an Upside-Down Horse**—hanging like a swing from a glass dome. David Černý, who created the statue in 1999, is one of the Czech Republic's most original contemporary artists. Always aspiring to provoke controversy, Černý has painted a menacing Russian tank pink, attached crawling babies to the rocket-like Žižkov TV tower, defecated inside the National Gallery to protest the policies of its director, and sank a shark-like Saddam Hussein inside an aquarium.

The grand staircase leading up from beneath the suspended sculpture takes you to a lavish 1930s Prague **cinema,** which shows mostly art-house films in their original language with Czech subtitles. The same staircase leads up to the swanky, Art Deco **Café Lucerna,** with windows overlooking this atrium. And in the basement, there's the popular **Lucerna Music Bar,** which hosts '80s and '90s video parties on weekends, and concerts on other nights (see page 179).

▸ *From the horse, turn right and head for the side exit (passing the entrance to the Lucerna Music Bar on your left). After you exit into the open air, jog a bit to the right across busy Vodičkova street (with a handy tram stop), where you'll find the entrance to the Světozor mall—it's a few steps to the right, by the* Kino *Světozor sign. Go on in.*

⑨ Světozor Mall

As you enter the mall, look up, at a glass window from the 1930s advertising Tesla, a now-defunct Czech radio manufacturer. The window lends a retro brightness to the place. On the left, pause at the always-busy Ovocný Světozor ("World of Fruit"), every local's favorite ice-cream joint (their specialty is banana-strawberry). They also sell cakes, milkshakes, and "little breads"—delightful Czech-style open-face sandwiches—really cheap. English menus are available on request. While licking your cone, ponder this: This nondescript space once housed the Theatre of the Seven Small Forms (known as the Semafor Theater), the center of the unprecedented creative outburst of the Czech culture that culminated in what became known as the Prague Spring.

▸ *Walk under the* Tesla *sign to leave the mall. As you exit, turn left immediately to enter the gates of the peaceful...*

⑩ Franciscan Garden

Ahhh! The garden's white benches and spreading rosebushes are a

Art Deco remnant in the Světozor Mall

Franciscan Garden, a New Town oasis

universe away from the fast beat of the city, which throbs behind the buildings corralling this little oasis.

The peacefulness reflects the purpose of its Franciscan origin. St. Francis, the founder of the order, thought God's presence could be found in nature. In the 1600s, Prague became an important center for a group of Franciscans from Ireland. Enjoy the herb garden and children's playground. (And a WC is just out the far side of the garden.) The park is a popular place for a discreet rendezvous; it's famous among locals for kicking off romances.

Looming up at the far end of the garden is a tall, truncated building that looks like it's been chopped in half. When the New Town was founded, its leaders commissioned **St. Mary of the Snows Church**—with its elegant white Gothic walls and lofty apse—to rival St. Vitus Cathedral, across the river. Like St. Vitus, construction halted with the religious wars of the 1400s; unlike St. Vitus, it never resumed. (If you want to peek inside, the entrance is just ahead, behind the Jungmann statue.)

▸ *Exit the garden at the opposite corner from where you entered (past the little yellow gardening pavilion—which now houses a design boutique—and the herb garden). You'll pass the handy pay WC, then pop out through a big gate into...*

⑪ Jungmann Square (Jungmannovo Náměstí)

The statue depicts **Josef Jungmann** (1773-1847), who revived the Czech language at a time when it was considered a simple peasants' tongue. To the left as you face Jungmann is the decadent, almost overly ornamented Adria Palace—which served as Václav Havel's "base camp" during those electrifying two weeks in November 1989.

Turn right past the statue, and follow the black paving stones as they cut through the skinny square. Ahead and on the right, look for the ⑫ **Baťa shoe store,** one of the big entrepreneurial success stories of pre-war Czechoslovakia. By making affordable but good-quality shoes, Tomáš Baťa's company thrived through the Depression years, only to be seized by the communists after World War II. The family moved their operation abroad, but have now reopened their factory in their hometown of Zlín. Today, Baťa shoes remain popular with Czechs—and international fashionistas.

Just to the right of the shoe store, near the corner of the square, notice the zigzag **Cubist lamppost**—one of many such flourishes scattered around this city. Just beyond the lamppost is a hidden beer garden that huddles around the base of the church.

▸ *Keep following those black paving stones through the glassed-in gallery next to the Baťa shoe store. You'll emerge near the bottom of Wenceslas Square.*

⑬ Můstek and the Old City Wall

The bottom of the Square marks the border between the Old Town and New Town. You'll notice the Metro stop Můstek, meaning "Bridge." You used to have to cross a bridge here, then pass through a fortified gate, to enter the Old Town, which was surrounded by a protective wall and moat. The Old Town and New Town were officially merged in 1784.

Let's finish the walk by bringing Czech history up to the moment. The Soviets were tossed out in the 1989 Velvet Revolution. Then the Czech Republic and Slovakia peacefully separated in the Velvet Divorce of 1993. Through the 1990s, the fledgling Czech Republic was guided by President Václav Havel, that former key-jingling playwright. In 2004, the Czech Republic became a member of the European Union. Today, Prague is home to more than one in ten Czechs. The Czech people, while not without problems, are enjoying a growing economy and a strong democracy. And Prague is understandably one of the most popular tourist destinations in Europe.

▸ *Our walk is done. Here at Můstek, you have many options: Continue straight ahead into the Old Town; turn right along Na Příkopě street (the former moat) to visit the Museum of Communism, Mucha Museum, or Municipal House; or go left along Národní street to the National Theater and the river. For places farther afield, you can hop on the Metro at Můstek. The rest of Prague is yours to enjoy.*

Prague Castle Tour

Pražský Hrad

For more than a thousand years, Czech leaders—from kings and emperors to Nazis, communists, and presidents—have ruled from Prague Castle. When Christianity arrived in the Czech lands, this promontory proved a perfect spot for a church. Later, the nobles built their palaces nearby, creating an elegant neighborhood that survives to this day.

This large complex contains a number of worthwhile sights: the castle itself (the grounds, gardens, and Old Royal Palace interior), St. Vitus Cathedral (stained glass and royal tombs), and a museum on the castle's history. With more time, you can step inside a number of historic sights and museums (such as Lobkowicz Palace) within the complex. Various combo-tickets cover some or all of these options.

If you plan to see these separate sights—the Strahov Monastery and Loreta Church (both covered in the Sights chapter)—it's easiest to visit them before the castle, since they're nearby and on the same hill.

ORIENTATION

Cost: Admission to the castle grounds is free, but you need a ticket to enter the sights. Most visitors choose "Circuit B" (250 Kč), which covers the highlights: St. Vitus Cathedral, the Old Royal Palace, the Basilica of St. George, and the Golden Lane. The more comprehensive "Circuit A" (350 Kč) adds a few sights, most notably The Story of Prague Castle exhibit (read the description on page 91 before investing in this ticket). Tickets are good for two days.

Hours: Castle sights—daily April-Oct 9:00-17:00, Nov-March 9:00-16:00, last entry 15 minutes before closing; castle grounds—daily 5:00-24:00. On Sunday, St. Vitus Cathedral is closed until noon for Mass. The cathedral can close unexpectedly for special services (check "events" at www.katedralasvatehovita.cz or call 724-933-441).

Buying Castle Tickets: There are three ticket offices (each marked by a green *"i"*): two in the Second Courtyard, and one in the Third Courtyard (in front of the cathedral). Lines can be long at one and nonexistent at the next, so if it's crowded, check all three. Hang on to your ticket; you must present it at each sight.

Crowd-Beating Tips: Prague Castle is one of the city's most crowded sights. Peak times are 9:30-12:30, especially May-Sept. Early birds should leave their hotel no later than 8:00 to be able to buy their ticket and be standing at the doors of St. Vitus Cathedral when they open at 9:00. Alternatively, arrive after 14:00, when crowds start subsiding (and leave crowded St. Vitus until the very end). At night, the sights are closed, but the grounds are free, floodlit, and atmospheric.

More Sights on and near the Castle Grounds: Additional sights at the castle are covered by their own, separate tickets, and have their own hours: the **St. Vitus Treasury in the Chapel of the Holy Cross** (300 Kč, daily 10:00-18:00, last entry one hour before closing) and climbing the **Great South Tower of St. Vitus Cathedral** (150 Kč, daily 10:00-18:30, until 16:30 in winter). Nearby sights include **Lobkowicz**

Palace (275 Kč, daily 10:00-18:00) and the **Toy Museum** (70 Kč, daily 9:30-17:30).

Information: Tel. 224-371-111, www.hrad.cz.

Tours: Hour-long **tours** in English depart from the main ticket office near the cathedral entrance about three times a day, but the basic tour covers only the cathedral and Old Royal Palace (100 Kč plus entry ticket, tourist.info@hrad.cz). You can rent a serviceable **audioguide** (350 Kč plus 500-Kč deposit).

Length of This Tour: Allow two to three hours for the castle complex. If you also visit the Strahov Monastery/Loreta Church or Lobkowicz Palace, allow an hour apiece.

Eateries: The castle complex has several forgettable cafés scattered within it, the best being the scenic, creative café at Lobkowicz Palace. Good eateries are located near the castle-complex exit (see page 151).

Starring: Europe's biggest castle, a fine cathedral with a stained-glass Mucha masterpiece, and grand views over the city.

Prague Castle is a 750,000 square-foot complex of palaces and courtyards. The entrance is just the tip of the iceberg.

Getting to Prague Castle

The tram is easy, or you could hike up, or take a taxi.

By Tram: Tram #22 takes you up to the castle (see page 126 for my self-guided tram tour, which ends at the castle). Catch it at one of these three convenient stops: the Národní Třída stop (between Wenceslas Square and the National Theater in the New Town); in front of the National Theater (Národní Divadlo, on the riverbank in the New Town); and at Malostranská (the Metro stop in the Little Quarter). Bring an extra ticket for the return trip to town, as there's no handy place to buy one at the castle.

After rattling up the hill, the tram makes three **stops** near the castle:

- **Královský Letohrádek** allows a scenic but slow approach through the Royal Gardens.
- **Pražský Hrad** is closest to the castle and the beginning of our tour. From the tram stop, simply walk along U Prašného Mostu and over the bridge, past the stonefaced-but-photo-op-friendly guards, and into the castle's Second Courtyard. Our tour begins nearby, on Castle Square.
- **Pohořelec** sits well uphill of the castle. It's not the best stop for the castle, but you could visit the Strahov Monastery, then walk 10 minutes downhill to the castle, stopping by Loreta Church on the way (see page 134).

By Taxi: If you tell your driver to take you to "the castle," the taxi ride is a long way around—and expensive. Instead, have the cab drop you off just under the castle at the top of Nerudova street and climb the cobblestones from there.

By Foot: The fairly steep, uphill, three-quarter-mile walk takes about 20 minutes from the river. From the Charles Bridge, follow the main cobbled road (Mostecká) to Little Quarter Square, marked by the huge, green-domed Church of St. Nicholas. (Alternatively, you could take the Metro to Malostranská, then walk down Valdštejnská street to Little Quarter Square.) From Little Quarter Square, hike uphill along Nerudova street. After about 10 minutes, a steep lane on the right leads to Castle Square—and the starting point for this tour. (If you continue straight, Nerudova becomes Úvoz and climbs to the Strahov Monastery.)

THE TOUR BEGINS

▶ *Start at Castle Square, which marks the west end of the huge complex.*
*You can't miss the **main entrance** to the castle: a gateway with a golden*
arch, guarded by two fighting-giant statues and two real-life soldiers in
their blue-and-white guardhouses.

❶ Castle Square (Hradčanské Náměstí)

You're standing at the tip of the medieval iceberg called Prague Castle. It's
a 1,900-foot-long series of courtyards, churches, and palaces, covering
750,000 square feet—by some measures, the largest castle on earth. In
the center of the complex sits St. Vitus Cathedral (the two prickly steeples
you see rising above the buildings).

The stoic **guards** at the main entrance make a great photo-op, as
does the changing of the guard (on the hour from 5:00-23:00). In fact,
there's a guard-changing ceremony at every gate: top, bottom, and side.
The best ceremony and music occurs at noon, at the top gate.

Now turn around and survey the broad expanses of Castle Square.

Enjoy the awesome city view and the entertaining bands that play
regularly at the gate. (If the Prague Castle Orchestra is playing, say hello
to friendly, mustachioed Josef, and consider buying the group's CD—it's
terrific.)

Castle Square was the focal point of medieval power. The archbishop
lived (and still lives) in the **Archbishop's Palace**—the ornate, white-and-
yellow Rococo palace on the right. Above the doorway is the coat of arms
of Prague's archbishops: three white goose necks in a red field.

On the left side of the square, the building with a step-gable roofline is

Photo-op with palace guard

Musicians perform regularly on Castle Square.

Prague Castle Quarter

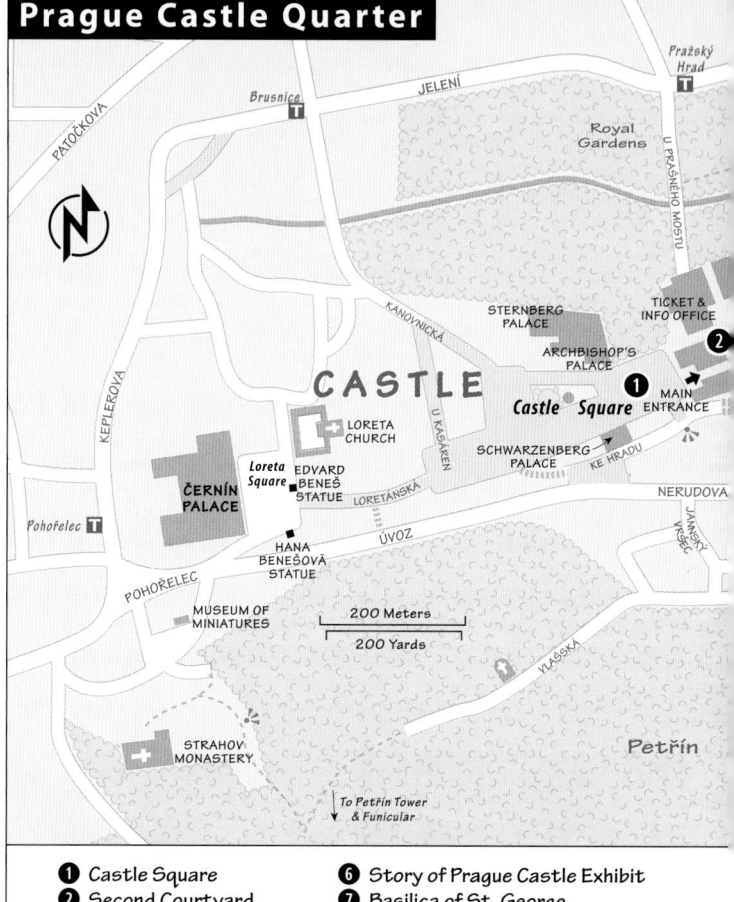

1 Castle Square
2 Second Courtyard
3 St. Vitus Cathedral
4 Third Courtyard
5 Old Royal Palace

6 Story of Prague Castle Exhibit
7 Basilica of St. George
8 Golden Lane
9 Lobkowicz Palace
10 Toy Museum

MARIÁNSKÉ HRADBY

Královský Letohrádek 🚇

ROYAL SUMMER PALACE

Chotkovy Park

BADENIHO

Letenské Park

ROYAL BALL GAME HALL

CHOTKOVA

NA OPYŠI

U BRUSKÝCH KASÁREN

Deer Moat

PRAGUE CASTLE

❽

❿

MAIN EXIT

STARÉ ZÁMECKÉ SCHODY (STAIRS)

Malostranská

❼

WC

Fürstenberg Gardens

❾

Pálffy Gardens

VALDŠTEJNSKÁ

🚇 🚇

U ŽELEZNÉ LÁVKY

❸

❺ WC

❹

❻ WC

TICKET & INFO OFFICE

PÁLFFY PALACE

POOL

Wallenstein Palace Garden

LION STATUE

WWII MONUMENT

MÁNESŮV MOST

Na Valech Gardens

QUARTER

ZÁMECKÉ SCHODY (STAIRS)

THUNOVSKÁ

TOMÁŠSKÁ

LETENSKÁ

Vojanovy Park Garden

CIHELNÁ

U LUŽICKÉHO SEMINÁŘE

CHURCH OF ST. NICHOLAS

Little Quarter Square

🚇 Malostranské Náměstí

ŘETISLAVOVA

VLAŠSKÁ

TRŽIŠTĚ

MOSTECKÁ

MÍŠEŇSKÁ

LITTLE QUARTER

TOWER ℹ️

SASKÁ

KARLŮV MOST

PROKOPSKÁ

ST. MARY THE VICTORIOUS

KARMELITSKÁ

NEBOVIDSKÁ

KÁŇSKÁ

LENNON WALL

Kampa Island

NA KAMPĚ

CHARLES BRIDGE

■ RIVER CRUISES

Hill

Vltava River

To Petřín Funicular ↓

Schwarzenberg Palace. Notice the envelope-shaped patterns stamped on the exterior. These Renaissance-era adornments etched into wet stucco—called sgraffito—decorate buildings throughout the castle and all over Prague.

The black Baroque sculpture in the middle of the square is a **plague column.** Erected as a token of gratitude to Mary and the saints for saving the population from epidemic disease, these columns are an integral part of the main squares of many Habsburg towns.

Closer to you, near the overlook, the statue of a man in a business suit (marked *TGM*) honors the father of modern Czechoslovakia: **Tomáš Garrigue Masaryk** (1850-1937). At the end of World War I, Masaryk—a former university prof and pal of Woodrow Wilson—united the Czechs and the Slovaks into one nation and became its first president. He was the only 20th-century leader to actually live inside Prague Castle.

▶ *Let's enter the castle. Walk through the golden gate, into the First Court-yard. Continue straight ahead, through the massive stone Matthias Gate (1614), where you'll emerge into the...*

❷ Second Courtyard

Straight ahead is the **Chapel of the Holy Cross.** This holds the St. Vitus Treasury exhibit, which displays precious old reliquaries and liturgical objects (covered by a separate ticket and skippable for most visitors).

Just to the left of the chapel, the modern green awning (with the golden-winged cat) marks the entrance to the **offices of the Czech president.**

Two **ticket offices** (with info desks) are in this courtyard, diagonally across from the chapel. You'll need a ticket for our next few sights, so buy one now. (If the ticket lines are long, continue into the Third Courtyard—our next stop—to see if the ticket office there is less busy.)

▶ *Now head for St. Vitus Cathedral. You'll walk through another passage-way and emerge into the Third Courtyard, facing the impressive facade of St. Vitus Cathedral.*

❸ St. Vitus Cathedral (Katedrála Sv. Víta)

This Roman Catholic cathedral is the Czech national church—it's where kings were crowned, royalty have their tombs, the relics of saints are venerated, and the crown jewels are kept. Since A.D. 930, a church has stood on this spot, marking the very origins of the Czech nation.

St. Vitus Cathedral, rising from the center of the castle complex, is where Czech kings have been crowned and buried.

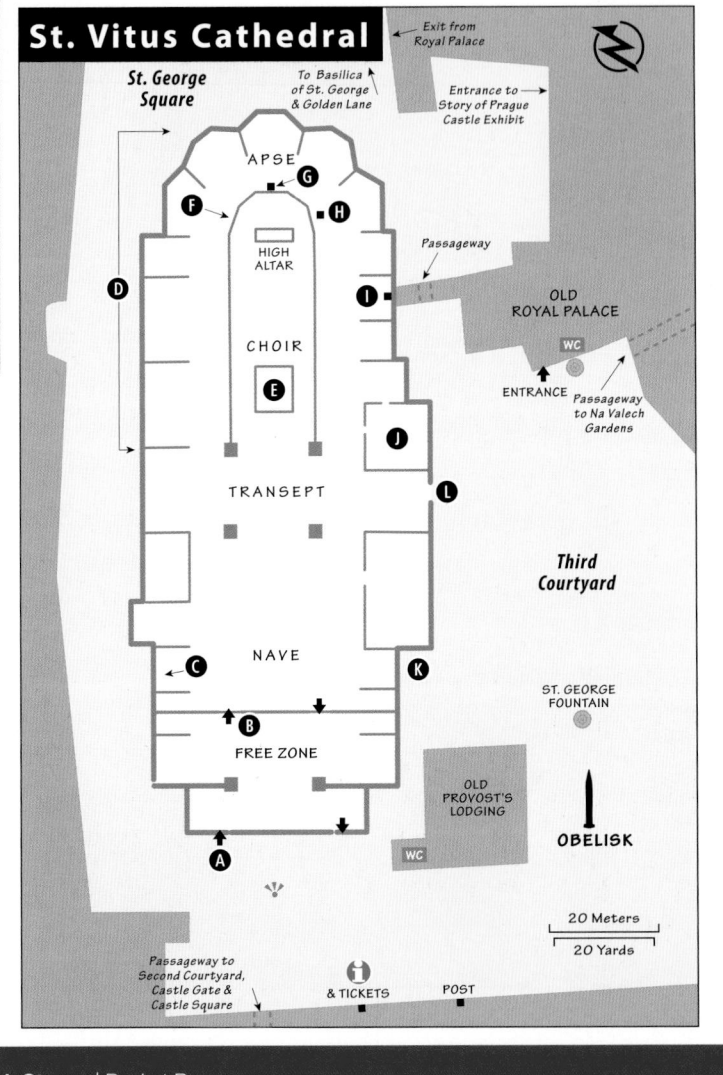

St. Vitus Cathedral

St. George Square

Exit from Royal Palace

To Basilica of St. George & Golden Lane

Entrance to Story of Prague Castle Exhibit

APSE

HIGH ALTAR

Passageway

OLD ROYAL PALACE

WC

ENTRANCE

Passageway to Na Valech Gardens

CHOIR

TRANSEPT

Third Courtyard

ST. GEORGE FOUNTAIN

NAVE

FREE ZONE

OLD PROVOST'S LODGING

WC

OBELISK

20 Meters

20 Yards

Passageway to Second Courtyard, Castle Gate & Castle Square

& TICKETS   POST

Ⓐ Entrance Facade
Ⓑ View Down the Nave
Ⓒ Mucha Stained-Glass Window
Ⓓ Old Church
Ⓔ Royal Mausoleum
Ⓕ Relief of Prague
Ⓖ Tomb of St. Vitus
Ⓗ Tomb of St. John of Nepomuk
Ⓘ Royal Oratory
Ⓙ Wenceslas Chapel
Ⓚ Tower Entrance
Ⓛ Last Judgment Mosaic

Ⓐ **Entrance Facade:** The two soaring towers of this Gothic wonder rise 270 feet. The ornate facade features pointed arches, elaborate tracery, Flamboyant pinnacles, a rose window, a dozen statues of saints, and gargoyles sticking their tongues out.

So what's up with the four guys in modern suits carved into the stone, as if supporting the big round window on their shoulders? They're the architects and builders who finished the church six centuries after it was started. Even though church construction got under way in 1344, wars, plagues, and the reforms of Jan Hus conspired to stall its completion. Finally, fueled by a burst of Czech nationalism, Prague's top church was finished in 1929 for the 1,000th Jubilee anniversary of St. Wenceslas. The entrance facade and towers were the last parts to be finished.

▶ *Enter the cathedral. If it's not too crowded in the (free-to-look) entrance area, work your way to the middle of the church for a good...*

Ⓑ **View Down the Nave:** The church is huge—more than 400 feet long and 100 feet high—and flooded with light. Notice the intricate "net" vaulting on the ceiling, especially at the far end. It's the signature feature of the church's chief architect, Peter Parler (who also built the Charles Bridge).

Tomb for royalty in a grand setting

The nave is 400 feet long.

▶ *Now make your way through the crowds and pass through the ticket turnstile (left of the roped-off area). The third window on the left wall is worth a close look.*

⦿ Mucha Stained-Glass Window: This masterful 1931 Art Nouveau window was designed by Czech artist Alfons Mucha and executed by a stained-glass craftsman (if you like this, you'll love the Mucha Museum in the New Town, and Mucha's masterpiece, *Slav Epic,* in Veletržní Palace).

Mucha's window was created to celebrate the birth of the Czech nation and the life of Wenceslas. The main scene (in the four central panels) shows Wenceslas as an impressionable child kneeling at the feet of his Christian grandmother, St. Ludmila. She spreads her arms and teaches him to pray. Wenceslas would grow up to champion Christianity, uniting the Czech people.

Above Wenceslas are the two saints who first brought Christianity to the region: Cyril (the monk in black hood holding the Bible) and his older brother, Methodius (with beard and bishop's garb). They baptize a kneeling convert.

Alfons Mucha—Prague's patriotic master of Art Nouveau—honored his nation with this stained-glass window.

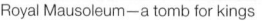

Modern stained-glass in the 20th-c. part of the church

Royal Mausoleum—a tomb for kings

Follow their story in the side panels, starting in the upper left. Around A.D. 860 (back when Ludmila was just a girl), these two Greek missionary brothers arrive in Moravia to preach. The pagan Czechs have no written language to read the Bible, so (in the next scene below), Cyril bends at his desk to design the necessary alphabet (Glagolitic, which later developed into Cyrillic), while Methodius meditates. In the next three scenes, they travel to Rome and present their newly translated Bible to the pope. But Cyril falls ill, and Methodius has to watch his kid brother die.

Methodius carries on (in the upper right), becoming bishop of the Czech lands. Next, he's arrested for heresy for violating the pure Latin Bible. He's sent to a lonely prison. When he's finally set free, he retires to a monastery, where he dies mourned by the faithful.

But that's just the beginning of the story. At the bottom center are two beautiful (classic Mucha) maidens, representing the bright future of the Czech and Slovak peoples. (And on the very bottom, the tasteful little ad for *Banka Slavie,* which paid for the work, is hardly noticeable.)

▶ *Continue circulating around the church, following the one-way, clockwise route.*

🅓 **The Old Church:** Just after the transept, notice there's a slight incline in the floor. That's because the church was actually constructed in two distinct stages. You're entering the older, 14th-century Gothic section. The front half (where you came in) is a Neo-Gothic extension that was finally completed in the 1920s (which is why much of the stained glass has a modern design). For 400 years—as the nave was being extended—a temporary wall kept the functional altar area protected from the construction zone.

▶ *In the choir area (on your right), soon after the transept, look for the big, white marble tomb surrounded by a black iron fence.*

Ⓔ Royal Mausoleum: This contains the remains of the first Habsburgs to rule Bohemia, including Ferdinand I, his wife Anne, and Maximilian II. The tomb dates from 1590, when Prague was a major Habsburg city.

▶ *Just after the choir, as you begin to circle around the back of the altar, watch on your right for the fascinating, carved-wood...*

Ⓕ Relief of Prague: This depicts the aftermath of the Battle of White Mountain, when the Protestant King Frederic escaped over the Charles Bridge (before it had any statues). Carved in 1630, the relief gives you a peek at old Prague. Find the Týn Church (far left) and St. Vitus Cathedral (far right), which was half-built at that time. The old city walls—now replaced by the main streets of the city—stand strong. The Jewish Quarter is the flood-prone zone along the riverside below the bridge on the left—land no one else wanted. The weir system on the river—the wooden barriers that help control its flow—survives to this day.

▶ *Circling around the high altar, you'll see various...*

Tombs in the Apse: Among the graves of medieval kings and bishops is that of **Ⓖ St. Vitus,** shown as a young man clutching a book and gazing up to heaven. Why is this huge cathedral dedicated to this rather obscure saint, who was martyred in Italy in A.D. 303 and never set foot in Bohemia? Because a piece of Vitus' arm bone was supposedly acquired by Wenceslas I in 925, and Wenceslas built a church here to house the relic and attract pilgrims. Vitus became quite popular throughout the Germanic and Slavic lands, and revelers danced on his feast day. (He's now the patron saint of dancers.) At the statue's feet is a rooster, because the saint

17th-century relief shows a "bridge" of weirs.

St. John of Nepomuk with halo of stars

was thrown into a boiling cauldron along with the bird (the Romans' secret sauce)...but the saint miraculously survived.

A few steps farther, the big silvery tomb with the angel-borne canopy honors ⒣ **St. John of Nepomuk.** Locals claim it has more than a ton of silver (for more on St. John of Nepomuk and his halo of stars, see page 39).

Just past the tomb, on the wall of the choir (on the right), is another finely carved, circa-1630 **wood relief** depicting an event that took place right here in St. Vitus: Protestant nobles trash the cathedral's Catholic icons after their (short-lived) victory.

Ahead on the left, look up at the ⒤ **royal oratory,** a box supported by busy late-Gothic, vine-like ribs. This private box, connected to the king's apartment by a corridor, let the king attend Mass in his jammies. The underside of the balcony is morbidly decorated with dead vines and tree branches, suggesting the pessimism common in the late Gothic period, when religious wars and Ottoman invasions threatened the Czech lands.

▶ *From here, walk 25 paces and look left through the crowds and door to see the richly decorated chapel containing the tomb of St. Wenceslas. Two roped-off doorways give visitors a look inside. The best view is from the second one, around the corner and to the left, in the transept.*

⒥ **Wenceslas Chapel:** This fancy chapel is the historic heart of the church. It contains the tomb of St. Wenceslas, patron saint of the Czech nation; it's where Bohemia's kings were crowned; and it houses (but rarely displays) the Bohemian crown jewels. The chapel walls are paneled with big slabs of precious and semiprecious stones. The jewel-toned stained-glass windows (from the 1950s) admit a soft light. The chandelier is exceptional. The place feels medieval.

The tomb of St. Wenceslas is a colored-stone coffin topped with an ark. Above the chapel's altar is a statue of Wenceslas, bearing a lance and a double-eagle shield. He's flanked by (painted) angels and the four patron saints of the Czech people. Above Wenceslas are portraits of Charles IV (who built the current church) and his beautiful wife. On the wall to the left of the altar, frescoes depict the saint's life, including the episode where angels arrive with crosses to arm the holy warrior. (For more on Wenceslas, see page 63.)

For centuries, Czech kings were crowned right here in front of Wenceslas' red-draped coffin. The new king was handed a royal scepter, orb, and sword, and fitted with the jeweled St. Wenceslas crown made for Charles IV. These precious objects are kept locked away behind a door in

The Wenceslas Chapel, with Wenceslas' tomb (right), is where Czech kings were crowned.

the corner of the chapel. The door (and the iron safe behind it) has seven locks whose seven keys are held by seven bigwigs (including the Czech president), who must all meet here when someone needs to get inside.

▶ Leave the cathedral, turn left (past the public WC), and survey the...

❹ Third Courtyard

The **obelisk** was erected in 1928—a single piece of granite celebrating the 10th anniversary of the establishment of Czechoslovakia and commemorating the soldiers who fought for its independence. It was originally much taller, but broke in transit—an inauspicious start for a nation destined to last only 70 years.

From here, you get a great look at the sheer size of St. Vitus Cathedral and its fat green **tower** (325 feet tall). Up there is the Czech Republic's biggest **bell** (16.5 tons, from 1549), nicknamed "Zikmund." In June 2002 it cracked, and two months later the worst flood in recorded history hit the city—the locals saw this as a sign. As a nation sandwiched between great powers, Czechs are deeply superstitious when it comes to the tides of history. You can view the bell as you climb up the 287 steps of the tower to the observation deck at the top (buy ticket and **Ⓚ** enter the tower near the sculpture of St. George—a 1960s replica of the 13th-century original).

It's easy to find the church's **Golden Gate** (for centuries the cathedral's main entry)—look for the glittering 14th-century mosaic of the **Ⓛ** Last Judgment. The modern, cosmopolitan, and ahead-of-his-time Charles IV commissioned this monumental decoration in 1370 in the Italian style. Jesus oversees the action, as some go to heaven and some go to hell. The Czech king and queen kneel directly beneath Jesus and six patron saints. On coronation day, royalty would walk under this arch, a reminder to them (and their subjects) that even those holding great power are not above God's judgment. See the grilled windows above this entryway? That's where the royal crown and national jewels are stashed.

▶ *In the corner of the Third Courtyard, near the copper awning, is the entrance to the Old Royal Palace. In the lobby, there's a WC with a window shared by the men's and women's sections—meet your partner to enjoy the view.*

❺ Old Royal Palace (Starý Královský Palác)

Since the ninth century, this has been the seat of the Bohemian princes. The highlight of the palace building (dating from the 12th century) is the large **Vladislav Hall**—200 feet long, with an impressive vaulted ceiling of vine-shaped (late-Gothic) tracery. This hall, used by the old nobility, served many purposes. It could be filled with market stalls, letting aristocrats shop without actually going into town. It was big enough for jousts—even the staircase (which you'll use as you exit) was designed to let a mounted soldier gallop in. Beginning in the 1500s, nobles met here to elect the king. The tradition survived into modern times. As recently as the 1990s, the Czech parliament crowded into this room to elect their president.

On your immediate right, enter the two small Renaissance rooms known as the **"Czech Office."** From these rooms (empty today except for their 17th-century porcelain heaters), two governors used to oversee the Czech lands for the Habsburgs in Vienna. Head for the far room, wrapped in windows. In 1618, angry Czech Protestant nobles poured into these rooms and threw the two Catholic governors out the window. An old law actually permits this act—called defenestration—which usually targets bad

The Old Royal Palace, with Vladislav Hall, is one of several sights you can pay to visit.

politicians. An old print on the glass panel shows the second of Prague's many defenestrations. The two governors landed—fittingly—in a pile of horse manure.

As you re-enter the main hall, go to the far end and out on the **balcony** for a sweeping view of Prague. Then head for the door immediately opposite. It opens into the **Diet Hall,** with a fine Gothic ceiling, a crimson throne, and benches for the nobility who once served as the high court. Notice the balcony on the left where scribes recorded the proceedings (without needing to mix with the aristocrats). The portraits on the walls depict Habsburg rulers, including Maria Theresa and Joseph II dressed up as George Washington (both wore the 18th-century fashions of the times), and the display case on the right contains replicas of the Czech crown jewels.

Return to the main hall; the next door to your right is the exit. Head down those horseback stairs. As you exit outside, pause at the door you just came through to consider the subtle yet racy little Renaissance knocker. Go ahead—play with it for a little sex in the palace (be gentle).

▶ *The next sight requires the "Circuit A" ticket; if you don't have one, skip down to the next stop.*

Otherwise, as you exit the Royal Palace, hook left around the side of the building and backtrack a few steps uphill to find stairs leading down to...

❻ The Story of Prague Castle Exhibit (Příběh Pražského Hradu)

This museum of old artifacts (with good English descriptions) is your best look at castle history and its kings, all housed in the cool Gothic cellars of the Old Royal Palace. Throughout the exhibit, models of the castle show how it grew over the centuries.

Origins (Room 1): In this low-ceilinged medieval room, you'll learn about prehistoric finds (mammoth bones) and the first settlers (c. 800), churches, and fortifications, and see ivory hunting horns of the first kings.

Patron Saints (Room 2): Czechs trace their origins as a people to several early saints. The first was St. Wenceslas, and you can admire (what may be) his actual chain-mail tunic and helmet. He was raised Christian by his grandmother, Ludmila (view her supposed clothes), and went on to found the original St. Vitus church. St. John of Nepomuk (no artifacts here) lies buried in the church's most ornate tomb.

Archaeological Finds (Room 3): Look through the metal floor to see the foundations of the 12th-century palace.

Golden Age of Bohemia (Room 4): In this large hall are numerous artifacts from 1200 through 1400. First comes the kings of the Přemysl family (including Ottokar II), then the dynasty of Charles IV and his IV wives.

Habsburg Rulers (Room 5): With Bohemia under Austrian rule, Prague declined. But Emperor Rudolf briefly moved the Habsburg court from Vienna to Prague (1583-1612), bringing with him current art styles (Mannerism—the transition from Renaissance to Baroque) and leading-edge scientists (astronomers Tycho Brahe and Johannes Kepler).

In this area, a display on the Czech coronation ceremony (always held in St. Vitus) includes fine replicas of the Bohemian crown jewels—scepter, orb, and crown (the originals are exhibited only on special occasions). They're a reminder that Prague Castle has been the center of the Czech state for more than a millennium.

▶ *Directly across the courtyard from the rear buttresses of St. Vitus is a very old church with a pretty red facade. This is the...*

❼ Basilica of St. George (Bazilika Sv. Jiří)

Step into one of the oldest structures at Prague Castle to see Prague's best-preserved Romanesque church and the burial place of Czech royalty. The church was founded by Wenceslas' dad around 920, and the present structure dates from the 12th century. (Its Baroque facade came later.) Inside, the place is beautiful in its simplicity. Notice the characteristic thick walls and rounded arches. In those early years, building techniques were not yet advanced enough to use those arches for the ceiling—it's made of wood instead.

This was the royal burial place before St. Vitus was built, so the tombs here contain the remains of the earliest Czech kings. Climb the stairs that frame either side of the altar to study the area around the apse. St. Wenceslas' grandmother, Ludmila, was reburied here in 925. Her stone tomb is in the space just to the right of the altar. Inside the archway leading to her tomb, look for her portrait. Holding a branch and a book, she looks quite cultured for a 10th-century woman.

▶ *Now continue walking downhill on that lane. You'll see the basilica's Romanesque nave and towers—a strong contrast to the pretty Baroque facade. Farther down, to the left, were the residences of soldiers and craftsmen, and to the right, tucked together, were the palaces of Catholic nobility who wanted both to be close to power and able to band together should the Protestants grab the upper hand. The next street on the left leads up to the popular Golden Lane. As you pass through the entry turnstiles, the crowds turn right, but don't overlook the sights to your left (including a tiny café).*

The red-hued Basilica of St. George   The basilica's interior retains a 12th-century feel.

❽ Golden Lane (Zlatá Ulička)

The tiny, old, colorfully painted buildings of this picturesque street origi-nally housed castle servants, and perhaps goldsmiths. Now they house displays on the olden days—medieval torture, alchemy, armor, medieval clothing—and re-creations of a classic pub and a goldsmith's workshop. Well-written English texts explain the history of the lane and its cannon towers, which served as prisons. Other small buildings are now gift shops selling old-timey products. At various points along the lane, you can climb up to a very cramped corridor that runs atop the houses; in this area, you'll find an armory and access to a tower with mediocre views (at the left end) and a measly torture collection (one cluttered room with unexplained tor-ture tools, near the WC, in the middle).

The houses themselves were occupied until World War II—Franz Kafka lived briefly (1916-1917) at #22, just to the right as you enter. Kafka moved in the year after publication of his most famous book, *The Metamorphosis* (elevator pitch: man wakes up as cockroach). A few years

The Golden Lane has pastel homes, gift shops, and exhibits on the medieval lifestyle.

after his time here, he wrote an (unfinished) book called *The Castle,* which may have been inspired by his own castle days.

At the bottom of the lane (past the last house, #12), tourists get flushed down a tight, stepped corridor. Before leaving, notice the tiny **cinema** room nearby that shows clips from classic Czech black-and-white films.

The Rest of the Castle

Our tour is over. But remember there are other sights to see in the complex—some free, some requiring a ticket.

You'll exit the Golden Lane near the ❾ **Lobkowicz Palace** (paintings, a Beethoven manuscript, and an aristocratic ambience; see page 132) and the ❿ **Toy Museum** (a century of teddy bears, old model trains, and a bevy of Barbies).

Leaving the Castle: Tourists squirt slowly through a fortified door at the bottom end of the castle. There are some incredible views of the city. From here, the 700-some steps lead down a steep lane called Staré Zámecké Schody ("Old Castle Stairs") directly back to the riverbank and the Malostranská tram/Metro stop. For a gentler descent, start heading down the steep lane. About 40 yards below the castle exit, a gate on the left leads you through a scenic vineyard and past the recommended Villa Richter restaurants (see page 151) to the tram/Metro stop.

Slav Epic **Tour**

This collection of 20 massive canvases, painted by the great Czech Art Nouveau artist Alfons Mucha, depicts momentous events in Slavic history. Located at Veletržní Palace, the *Slav Epic* is one of the most powerful artistic experiences in Europe. It's easily worth ▲▲▲—don't miss it. Allow two hours to appreciate this masterpiece.

ORIENTATION

Cost: 180 Kč. A 240-Kč combo-ticket also includes the National Gallery's huge modern art collection in the same building.
Hours: Tue-Sun 10:00-18:00, closed Mon.

Getting There: The blocky, concrete, seemingly misnamed Veletržní "Palace" is located near Holešovice train station at Dukelských Hrdinů 47 (Praha 7; enter under the lion). To get there, catch a **tram** from any of the following stops to the Veletržní Pálac stop, which is right in front of the building: tram #17 from Národni Divadlo or Staroměstská (five/four stops); tram #24 from Náměstí Republiky (three stops); or tram #12 from Malostranská (three stops). The nearest **Metro** stop is Vltavská; exiting the Metro, walk through the underpass to the right of tram tracks, continue to the first tram intersection, turn right, and walk two blocks.

Information: An excellent 10-Kč English guide to the *Slav Epic* is available right in the gallery with the paintings. Tel. 224-301-122, www. ngprague.cz.

While You're There: Upstairs from the *Slav Epic* is the National Gallery's modern art collection, with works by Van Gogh, Picasso, and others, including their Czech contemporaries.

Length of This Tour: At least one hour (or up to two, for those who want to linger over the many details).

Photography: Photos permitted without flash.

Starring: A stunning artistic achievement, and a powerful history lesson about a major—and often overlooked—European culture.

Background

Alfons Mucha (1860-1939) was born in the small Moravian town of Ivančice. He studied in Vienna and Munich, and worked for a while in Moravia, and then—like most artists of his generation—he went to Paris to seek his fortune. After suffering as a starving artist, he was hired to design a poster for a play starring the well-known French actress Sarah Bernhardt. Overnight, Mucha was famous. He forged an instantly recognizable style: willowy maidens with flowing hair amid flowery designs and backed with a halo-like circle. His pastel pretties appeared on magazine covers, wallpaper, carpets, and ad campaigns hawking everything from biscuits to beer. Mucha's florid style helped define what became known as Art Nouveau.

But even as he pursued a lucrative (if superficial) career in Paris and the US, Mucha was always thinking about his native land. While preparing the Bosnian Pavilion for the Paris Exposition of 1900, he traveled widely through Slavic lands. He soaked up the culture, history, and proud

Alfons Mucha, the toast of turn-of-the-century Paris, returned to his homeland to create the *Slav Epic*.

traditions—and was inspired by the parallels he saw between the Czech narrative and the histories of fellow Slavic peoples. Inspired to immortalize great moments in Slavic history on a grand, epic scale, Mucha convinced the Chicago industrialist Charles Crane to bankroll his project. They both believed art could instill understanding and bring humanity closer together. The idealistic Mucha was determined to illuminate the little-known world of the Slavs for people everywhere.

At age 50—after years of living abroad—Mucha returned to his homeland and started work. For his studio, he rented a chateau that was big enough to accommodate the huge canvases. For the next 16-plus years, he cranked out these enormous works. He traveled far and wide throughout the Slavic world to do research and gain inspiration—Warsaw, Moscow, Dalmatia (near Dubrovnik), Macedonia...this truly was a pan-Slavic undertaking. At the same time, he was juggling fatherhood and the worries of World War I. The year 1918 brought a watershed in Czech history, as World War I ended and the modern self-governing nation of Czechoslovakia was created. Mucha was immediately tapped by the new government to design the nation's currency and stamps.

In 1928, on the 10th anniversary of modern Czechoslovakia, Mucha's lifework was finally unveiled. The response was lukewarm. In the experimental age of Picasso, Mucha's representational style was out of fashion. And with the rise of fascism in the 1930s, Mucha's overt Slavic nationalism came under attack. Outside of Slavic lands, people were (exactly as Mucha had feared) uninterested in the murky Slavic history he so earnestly celebrated. Historians scoffed at his oversimplified and often rosy-eyed take on this complex subject. Ever the perfectionist, Mucha continued to tinker with and rework details in his "completed" masterpiece for the rest of his life.

In 1939, German tanks rumbled into Czechoslovakia. The Nazis considered Slavs an inferior race. They arrested the patriot Mucha—now 79 years old—and he was interrogated by the Gestapo. He died a few weeks later.

During World War II, Mucha's canvases were rolled up and hidden away from the Nazis and, in the process, damaged. In 1963, after years of restoration, the paintings were put on display in the obscure Czech town of Moravský Krumlov, near Mucha's birthplace; then, in 2011, they were brought to Prague's Veletržní Palace. Mucha's work is finally in an accessible place where Czechs and tourists alike can appreciate his grand vision.

THE TOUR BEGINS

In these 20 panels, Mucha traces the 1,500-year history of the Slavic people. The panels are roughly chronological, but Mucha isn't above veering from the facts to emphasize the people's spiritual journey. While about half of the scenes are specifically Czech, and the rest are from other Slavic cultures, Mucha intended the themes illustrated to be universal, evoking not just Slavic but all human experience. The canvases are mind-bogglingly big—some are 25 by 20 feet, and together they total 6,800 square feet, slightly more than Michelangelo's Sistine ceiling. Mucha's magnum opus has been scorned by many Czech intellectuals for its style and overt patriotism. But the work goes beyond the style of the time, beyond Art Nouveau, and beyond Slavic nationalism.

▶ *Enter the spacious* Epic *hall. The paintings are gathered in five groups, which are (very loosely) united thematically.*

First Group

This series of three paintings focuses on the origins of the Slavic people and their enduring faith—both pagan and (later) Christian.

1. *The Slavs in Their Original Homeland* (1912)

It's A.D. 500. Nomadic tribes are sweeping across the European landscape—Huns from the East and Barbarians (Germanic tribes) from the West. The flames of a burning village consume the left horizon. Caught in the crossfire is a small population of peasants in today's Ukraine—the Slavs. They share a common language, culture, and DNA, but have no country to call their own. Occupying a "mysterious" (to Western Europeans)

The Slavs—Europe's eternal refugees

Svantovít—the Slavs' pagan roots

land at the fringe of the "civilized" world—wedged between the Christian West and the Muslim East—the Slavs have seen more than their share of invaders from both sides.

Two desperate refugees (at bottom) huddle for safety as their homeland is ravaged by invading armies (in the distance). The sickle here suggests that the Slavs are peace-loving farmers rather than warlike conquerors.

But from these humble beginnings, the Slavic people will someday rise to greatness—as symbolized by the vision of a pagan Slavic priest (upper right), acting as a sort of oracle for the journey to come. This figure hints at the mysticism that underlies the Slavic faith (particularly Orthodox Christianity). His arms are outstretched in a Christ-like pose (which you'll see repeated again and again throughout the *Epic*). Some Slavs have called themselves "the Christ of the Nations" for the way they have been continually persecuted by their powerful neighbors (Germans, Austrians, Huns, Ottoman Turks, and so on).

Mucha begins his 20-canvas story with this Slavic Adam and Eve driven from paradise. Over the centuries, the Slavs would roam from their Ukrainian epicenter, searching for a homeland in places as far away as (today's) Russia, Poland, the Balkans, and—on the western perimeter—Prague.

Mucha (an avid photographer) uses a double-exposure technique to show two realities: the historical/earthly events (the terrified couple and army) and the mythic otherworld (the priest flanked by symbols of "war" and "peace"). Also notice how Mucha highlights crucial details (like the couple's terrified faces) by using sharp-focus oil paints on top of the foggy—almost glittery—base of egg tempera.

2. *The Celebration of Svantovít* (1912)

In this swirling mass of white-robed figures, the Slavs gather to celebrate the harvest before the fertility god Svantovít (holding a drinking horn). While this theme captures the specific rituals of the Baltic Slavs, it evokes the deeply rooted traditions of pagan Slav-land. Blissed-out dancers sway in a trance, swinging linden branches. Hovering above, their gods join them. The Slavs are sacrificing bulls to Svantovít. But their peace is about to be shattered, in the form of Thor (upper left), who arrives with wolves. It's the Slavs' eternal enemy—the Germanic tribes.

When you gaze into the eyes of the forlorn-looking young mother (at bottom center, echoing the woman in the first painting), it seems that the Slavs are forever destined to be refugees.

3. *Introduction of the Slavonic Liturgy* (1912)

A boy with a ring introduces us to the next step in the Slavs' evolution—conversion to Christianity, thanks to St. Methodius (standing just left of center, with long white beard) and St. Cyril (in the background at left, leading a parade of men). Cyril and Methodius are unifying figures throughout the Slavic world (not to mention in Mucha's stained-glass window at St. Vitus Cathedral—see page 80). These Greek missionary brothers translated the Bible for their new converts, and even jump-started Slavic literacy by creating an alphabet to capture the tongue-twisting Slavic languages. A variation on that alphabet—Cyrillic, named for the saint who invented it—is still widely used.

Floating above the earthly scene, the Catholic pope and the Orthodox patriarch—representing the two strains of Slavic Christianity—embrace. But in the top left, in a menacingly dark scene, a pope and a Holy Roman Emperor preside over a forced baptism—a reminder that the Slavs didn't always accept Christ by choice. At the top right, flattened like Orthodox icons, are two ruler-couples (one Russian and the other Bulgarian) who welcomed the new religion of Christianity.

Second Group

This series focuses on strong medieval rulers who advanced the Slavic cause through education, law, and cooperation with neighboring states. These rulers—and others like them—established sophisticated kingdoms of art and literature across Eastern Europe.

Slavonic Liturgy—the Slavs become Christian

Tsar Simeon leads a Slavic renaissance.

4. *Tsar Simeon I of Bulgaria* (1923)

The enlightened Slavic ruler sits on his throne, dictating the Christian message to a scribe, who scrambles to write it all down. Other scholars in the foreground are busy studying and translating Byzantine classics into the Slavic tongue. The wisdom seems to radiate out from the center of this essentially circular composition—a series of radiating arches.

5. *King Přemysl Ottokar II of Bohemia* (1924)

In an elaborate tent set up for an outdoor wedding, King Ottokar (in shining gold, with a red cap) shakes hands to welcome royal guests from around Europe. By sealing political alliances with this marriage, Ottokar (c. 1233-1278) ushers in the Golden Age of Bohemia (i.e., the Czech lands).

6. *Coronation of the Serbian Tsar Stefan Dušan as East Roman Emperor* (1923)

A parade of happy Slavs leaves a church in Skopje (in today's Macedonia) after watching Stefan Dušan crowned as ruler of Serbia. Dušan (c. 1308-1355, just right of center, in the golden crown) was a strong leader. He introduced a code of law borrowed from Byzantium to govern his unruly subjects.

    As it happened, the golden days of Slavic self-rule were numbered. By the 14th century, Slavic lands were increasingly dominated by Germanic colonizers and by the Roman Catholic Church. Who could stand up to them?

Third Group

This section focuses on warfare, most of it fueled by religion—especially

King Ottokar forged peaceful alliances.

Tsar Dušan—celebrating all things Slavic

Jan Milíč—a Czech reformer

Battle of Grunwald—Slavs vs. Germans

the Catholics-versus-Protestants wars that wracked the Czech lands. (The painting numbers below aren't sequential, but view the canvases in this order.)

8. *After the Battle of Grunwald* (1924)

On July 15, 1410, a Slavic army squared off against the fearsome Teutonic Knights (Germanic former Crusaders trying to take over the Baltic Coast). The Slavs held out. The battlefield is littered with the blood-stained tunics (white with black crosses) of the Teutonic Knights. And yet, notice how Mucha doesn't show the winners reveling in victory; instead, their faces express sorrow over the destruction and loss of life.

7, 9-10. *The Magic of Words* Triptych (1916)

This three-paneled work—the kind normally seen as a church altarpiece—is dedicated to the life and influence of the great Czech reformer who spoke truth to power, Jan Hus. (For more on Hus, see page 17.)

 7. *Jan Milíč of Kroměříž* (left panel): Jan Milíč, one of Hus' charismatic predecessors as a people's preacher, inspired repentance even among society's downtrodden. Here, a notorious brothel in Prague's Old Town has been dismantled and is now being replaced with a convent for reformed prostitutes. The singing girls shed their jewelry for white cloaks just because of Milíč's persuasive words.

 9. *Master Jan Hus Preaching at Bethlehem Chapel* (central panel): The scene is Bethlehem Chapel, 1414. Hus preaches from the pulpit (left), leaning out to make his point. He's been excommunicated by the pope for his heretical views. But here in Prague he's a rock star. Among the rapt listeners are other major figures in the drama: The queen, listening

Jan Hus preaching—the Prague professor inspired the Czechs with religious reform and nationalism

intently, sits at far right (under a canopy, wearing a white dress and red crown). On the far left, standing against a wall, is General Jan Žižka (with a long mustache and an eye patch), the future military leader of the Hussites. But there's a weasel in their midst—directly in front of the queen, a lady-in-waiting directs a quizzical look toward a caped figure (at the far right), furiously taking notes. With the damning "evidence" of this spying priest, in a few short weeks, Hus would be arrested, imprisoned, and eventually burned at the stake.

But his legacy lived on...

10. *The Meeting at Křížky* (right panel): On a remote hill outside Prague, Hus' followers gather as they prepare to defend their beliefs. The Hussite Wars are coming. The sky darkens.

11. *After the Battle of Vítkov Hill* (1923)

War comes to Prague. In this battle (1420), on a hill east of Prague's Old Town, the Hussites drove off the pope's forces. Now a priest holds a monstrance and says Mass—a service that will include both the bread and the wine, affirming the fundamental right the Hussites were fighting for. Amid the gloom, a glimmer of heavenly light shows through and illuminates General Jan Žižka, who thanks God for the victory.

12. *Petr Chelčický* (1918)

Refugees from the wars—in this case, victims of Hussite atrocities—flee their village. One angry man (near the center) turns and vows revenge, but he's restrained by peace-loving Petr (in hat and scarf and clutching a Bible). Petr's pacifist ideas would later inspire Comenius and the Unity of the Brethren (see #15 and #16, later), Tolstoy, and Mucha himself. Although historically specific, this painting captures the universality of the refugee experience.

Fourth Group

This cycle of canvases features the benchmarks and growing pains of the Slavs in modern times.

13. *The Hussite King Jiří z Poděbrad* (1923)

At war's end, the pope and the Hussites signed a peace treaty allowing the Czechs to choose their own king. But this scene—set in Prague's Old Town Hall, framed by a stained glass window—makes it clear that the long fight for Slavic autonomy isn't over. The pope's ambassador (in red, framed by the window) tries to weasel out of the deal. The proud Czech king (far right) stands up and defies the pope by kicking over the ambassador's chair. The king is so mighty that he bows to no one, not even the pope's representative. The young boy in the front is one of Mucha's self-portraits.

Petr Chelčický (in hat) aids refugees.

Hussite King Jiří signs a peace treaty.

The *Slav Epic* and World War I

While some of Mucha's war paintings were painted after World War I (1914-1918), many were executed against the backdrop of the horrors of this war. Compare the give-'em-hell jingoism of prewar battle scenes (*The Defense of Szigetvár by Nikola Zrinski*, done just before war broke out in 1914) with the cynical revenge of war's end (*Petr Chelčický*, 1918), to the solemn reflection about death that settled in after the war (*After the Battle of Grunwald*, 1924).

The treaty painting (*The Hussite King Jiří z Poděbrad*, 1923) resonates with the Treaty of Versailles that ended that war. That accord created new Slavic nations in Europe (Czechoslovakia, Hungary, Poland), but their autonomy was constantly threatened by more powerful forces around them.

Ultimately, Mucha became a pacifist, convinced that the only longlasting hope for the Slavic peoples lay in the power of knowledge and spiritual enlightenment.

14. *The Defense of Szigetvár by Nikola Zrinski* (1914)

This fiery red canvas shows how the Slavs also had to defend their lands against Muslim Ottomans. As the Ottomans encroached on European territory—at one point even knocking on Vienna's city gates—all of Europe looked to the Slavs and Hungarians as the last line of defense. Szigetvár—a small town in southern Hungary—was a Central European Alamo. Outnumbered 50 to 1, the defenders vowed to go up in flames for their cause. They did. A column of black smoke rises up ominously in the foreground. In the upper right, a Czech noblewoman prepares to light the fuse on this tower of gunpowder.

15. *The Brethren School in Ivančice* (1914)

After so much bloodshed, this scene is refreshingly positive and optimistic. We're in a garden outside the city wall of Ivančice, Mucha's hometown (near Brno, 150 miles southeast of Prague). The teenager at lower right (in white shirt, carrying a sheaf of papers) is Mucha himself.

Ivančice was home to a band of pacifists called the Unity of the Brethren, who put into practice the ideas of Petr Chelčický (see #12,

Defense of Szigetvár—the Slavic Alamo

Jan Komenský—educator and patriot

earlier). They helped bring literacy to the Slavic lands by translating the Latin Bible into what would become (for the next couple of centuries) the standard written language of the Czech lands and Slovakia. Their actions helped keep the Czech language alive.

The wooden lean-to on the right is the Bible print shop. Mucha is bringing in fresh paper to help spread the good word. Rich and poor alike intermingle, showing the leveling effect of education.

16. *Jan Amos Komenský* (1918)
On a lonely seashore sits a solitary figure. It's the famous Czech teacher John Amos Comenius (Jan Amos Komenský in Czech, 1592-1670), the man who virtually invented textbooks and modern education. Now at the end of his days—having lived as an exile for his beliefs—he faces death alone. His followers huddle nearby. Will they ever regain their homeland? The tiny lantern holds out "A Flicker of Hope" (Mucha's subtitle for the work).

Fifth Group
The final set of paintings provides a stirring climax. After focusing on lots of specific historical events, Mucha—now in his sixties and nearing completion of the cycle—circles back to some of the themes of what makes Slavs Slavs. In these canvases, notice the return of the double-exposure mysticism of early works. That mysticism is a key component of Slavic faith—particularly Eastern Orthodox Christianity, professed by the eastern half of the Slavic lands.

17. *The Holy Mount Athos* (1926)

The scene is an Orthodox church, lit by shafts of light. Pilgrims fill the church below while holy presences inhabit the sunlit atmosphere above. Orthodox worship is designed to create a transformative—or even hallucinatory—state: Worshippers stand through the service, inhale heavy incense, and focus all their attention on glittering icons.

Before making this piece, Mucha visited the Orthodox monastery of Mount Athos, in Greece—a pilgrimage center for Orthodox Slavs. Though very much a worldly, modern man, Mucha was fascinated by occult forms of Christianity. He saw Christianity as a unifying and enlightening element for the Slavic people.

18. *The Oath of the Youth Under the Slavic Linden Tree* (1926)

But Mucha never neglected the Slavs' pagan origins. Here, young people join hands to sing "Kumbaya." There are those Christ poses again—but this time, joined in unity. They are paying homage to the goddess of their people, Slávia, who sits in the boughs of a linden tree (an important symbol to Slavic people).

Men in 19th-century clothes join in. They're part of the national revival movement in the 1800s to celebrate Slavic language and culture, and create a homeland. Starting in the mid-1800s, after centuries of living under mighty empires, the various Slavic groups (and other underdog nationalities) began to band together and celebrate the things that made each one unique.

The work remains unfinished—many faces are only sketches, and there's a mysterious cloud in the center. Though the faces are left anonymous, they could easily be men like Antonín Dvořák and Bedřich Smetana,

Oath of Youth—remembering pagan roots

Abolition of Serfdom—a boon for Slavs

who composed symphonies from folk songs to remind the Slavic peoples of their common heritage. The two allegorical figures sitting on the wall are Mucha's son and daughter.

19. *The Abolition of Serfdom in Russia* (1914)

In Moscow's Red Square, the Russian proclamation that freed the serfs has just been issued (1861). Stunned by the news that their slaves are now free, the populace wanders dumbfounded across a snowy field. The symbols of Russian oppression—the Kremlin and St. Basil's Cathedral—loom behind. Emancipation is a first step for a few Slavs, but true freedom for all remains a dream.

   To research this canvas, Mucha traveled to Russia on the heels of the Bolshevik Revolution. The freeing of the serfs led to massive unemployment, which helped spark the communist revolution, which—ironically—led to the next, grim chapter in the history of the Slavs: the takeover of the entire Slavic world by the Soviet Union following World War II.

20. *Apotheosis "Slavs for Humanity!"* (1926)

An "apotheosis" is the elevation of someone or something to divine status, and in this case, it's the Slavs. In this final panel, Mucha tries to sum up the entire 1,500-year journey of the Slavic people and predict where they're headed. Take a deep breath and dive in.

   Start in the lower right. In blue, we see the huddled, oppressed people of the sixth century longing for a peaceful homeland. In the upper left (the band of red), it's the Middle Ages, and the Slavs rise to prominence under a series of strong kings (like the man on his throne to the right).

   In the center (joyous yellow), it's 1918. World War I has ended, and gaily clad Slavs rejoice, waving flags of the victorious nations (including the Stars and Stripes) and olive branches to salute the troops. Emerging from the war is a new Slavic nation—Czechoslovakia—symbolized by the (Christ-like) torso of a strong young man who rises up from the chaos, clutching the wreaths of freedom and Slavic unity. Behind him, the actual Christ blesses the new nation, and a rainbow signals a new era of peace.

   Today, the Slavic community is almost 400 million strong. They inhabit the Czech Republic, Slovakia, Poland, much of the Balkans, Ukraine, Belarus, Russia, and beyond—including 18 million Slavic Americans. Some are Catholic, some Orthodox; some write in Cyrillic script, some

Apotheosis—Mucha's glorious last panel depicts the Czech nation as a vibrant young man on the rise.

Latin. But they share a common heritage, which Mucha has celebrated in the audacious artistic endeavor known as the *Slav Epic*.

► *Behind the final partition, a video monitor shows a loop of three **films** (nearly two hours total) about the work and the quest to return it to Prague (English subtitles).*

*If you have the interest (and paid extra for the combo-ticket), consider the rest of the museum. Start on floor 4 and work down (roughly chronologically) through a spacious, never-crowded display of Czech masters from the 19th century to the present. On floor 3 (among the Czech art), look for **The Collection of French Art,** with a handful of masterpieces by Van Gogh (Green Corn), Toulouse-Lautrec (Moulin Rouge), Henri Rousseau (Self-Portrait), Picasso (Standing Women and Self-Portrait 1907), and lesser works by well-known Impressionists.*

Sights in Prague

These sights are arranged by neighborhood for handy sightseeing. Remember that Prague started out as four towns—the Old Town and New Town on the east side of the river, and the Castle Quarter and Little Quarter on the west—and it's still helpful for sightseers to think of the city that way. I've also included a pair of worthwhile sights outside of the city center.

When you see a ✪ in a listing, it means the sight is covered in much more depth in one of the self-guided walk or tour chapters.

Unlike some cities, Prague does not have a must-get sightseeing pass that covers the major sights. Check www.ricksteves.com/update for any significant changes that have occurred since this book was published. For tips on sightseeing, see page 173.

Prague Sights

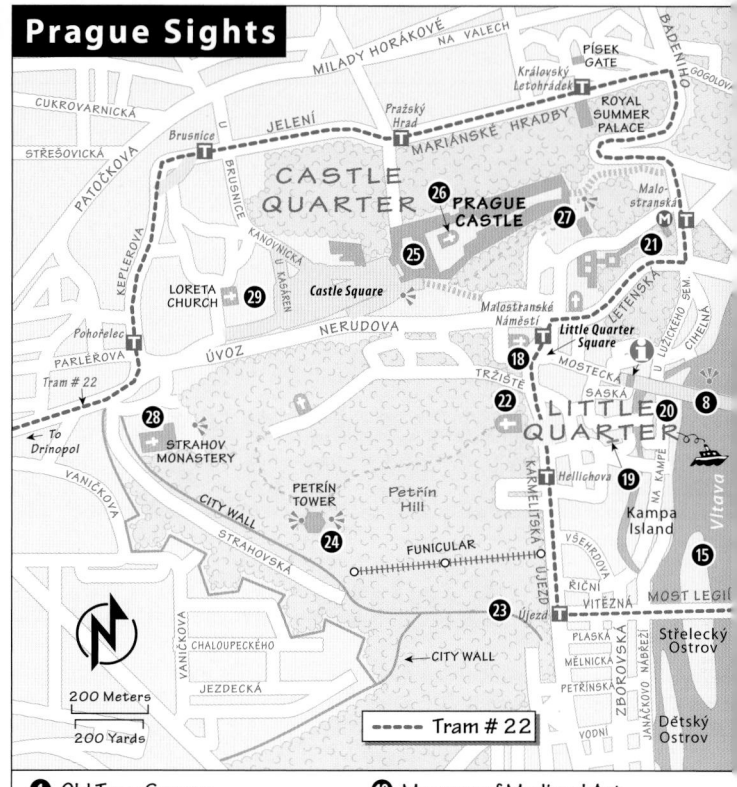

1. Old Town Square
2. Old Town Hall Tower
3. Church of St. Nicholas
4. Týn Church
5. Church of St. James
6. Havelská Market
7. Klementinum
8. Charles Bridge
9. Jewish Quarter
10. Museum of Medieval Art
11. Wenceslas Square & Nat'l Museum
12. Mucha Museum
13. Museum of Communism
14. Municipal House & Powder Tower
15. Vltava River: Boats & Beaches
16. Tram #22 to Prague Castle
17. To the National Memorial–Heydrich Terror

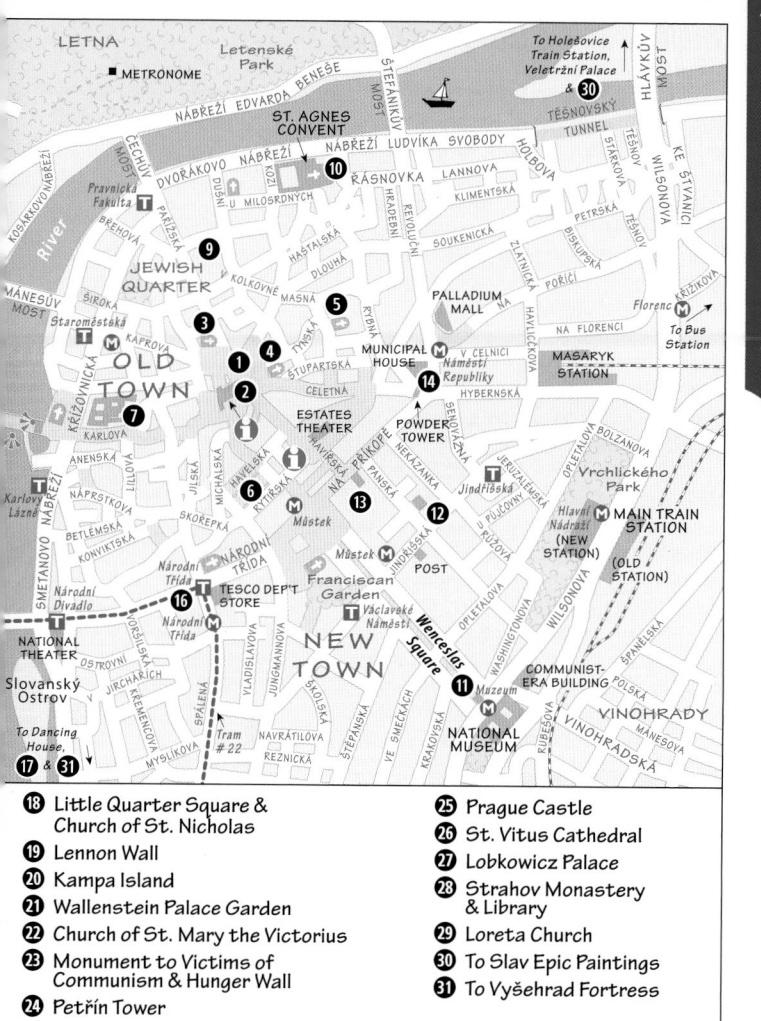

THE OLD TOWN (STARÉ MĚSTO)

All of the sights described here are within a 10-minute walk of the magnificent Old Town Square. For a self-guided tour of the square and its main landmarks, see the ✪ Old Town Walk chapter.

▲▲▲Old Town Square (Staroměstské Náměstí)

Prague's Old Town Square—a perfectly preserved living postcard—is the focal point of most tourist visits. The central statue, a memorial to Jan Hus, is surrounded by an architectural parade of picturesque buildings, including the Old Town Hall.

✪ See the Old Town Walk chapter.

Old Town Hall Tower and Tour

The town hall building hosts Prague's main TI (and has WCs). But the most popular feature is on the outside—its ludicrously complex, wheels-within-wheels Astronomical Clock. ✪ For an explanation of what makes this mysterious clock tick, see the Old Town Walk chapter.

You can take an elevator to the top of the town hall's ▲▲ tower for views over Prague's prettiest square. Or take a 45-minute guided tour of the town hall's Gothic interior and a close-up look at the inner workings of the Astronomical Clock.

Tower: Enter through the door immediately to the left of the clock, then ride the elevator to floor 3 to buy your ticket, where you catch another elevator to the top (110 Kč, Tue-Sun 9:00-21:00, Mon 11:00-21:00; after 19:00, enter through door immediately left of the clock).

Guided Tour of Interior: Enter at TI, then ascend to floor 1 to sign

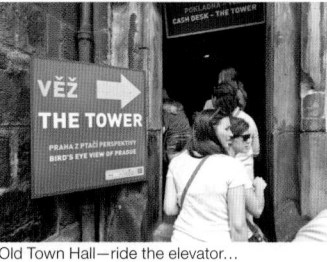

Old Town Hall—ride the elevator…

…to a great view over the the Old Town Square and city.

up for next tour (100 Kč, or 160-Kč combo-ticket with tower, about 3 tours/day in English—see the schedule at the ticket desk).

▲Týn Church

The twin, multiturreted, fairy-tale-like Gothic towers of the Church of Our Lady Before Týn (its full name) loom over the Old Town Square. While every tourist snaps a photo of this church, consider stepping inside, too.

The Týn Church (pronounced "teen") is the Old Town's main church. It has roots back to the 1100s, though this structure dates from Prague's Golden Age, built around 1360 as the university church (by the same architect who did St. Vitus Cathedral at Prague Castle). The fanciful **steeples** (with their forest of sub-steeples) aren't exactly "twins"—they were built a century apart, and one is slightly fatter.

Enter (through a cluster of buildings in front of it) at #14. The structure is full of light, with soaring Gothic arches. The interior reflects the church's complex history. First it was Catholic. Then the Hussites (Protestants) white-washed and stripped it of Catholic icons. When the Catholic Habsburgs retook it, they encrusted it with noisy Baroque altars, statues of Mary and the saints, and black-and-gold highlights.

Týn Church's varied interior reflects the city's history as both Hussite and Catholic.

Circle the interior counterclockwise. Midway up the right aisle, find an exquisite carved-wood Baptism-of-Christ **altarpiece.**

At the front-right corner of the church, on the pillar to your right is a brown stone slab showing a man in armor with a beard and ruff collar, his hand resting on a globe. This is **Tycho Brahe** (1546-1601), the first modern astronomer, who worked in Prague.

Continue on to face the stunning **main altar,** topped with a statue of an angel with a flaming sword. A painting (on the lower level) shows Mary ascending to heaven where (in the next painting up) she's to be crowned. To the right of the altar is a statue of one of Prague's patron saints—John of Nepomuk (wearing his halo of stars; see page 39).

You're surrounded by the **double-eagle symbol** of the Catholic Habsburgs: on the flag borne by a knight statue on the altar, atop the organ behind you (Prague's oldest), and above you on the ceiling.

Exploring the rest of the church, you'll see lots of reliefs of knights who are buried underfoot, and a number of "marble" altarpieces that are (knock, knock) actually made of wood.

30-Kč requested donation, generally open to sightseers Tue-Sat 10:00-13:00 & 15:00-17:00, Sun 10:30-12:00, closed Mon. No photos.

▲Church of St. James (Kostel Sv. Jakuba)

Fine old medieval church redecorated head-to-toe in exuberant Baroque, and its main relic, the Madonna Pietatis.

✪ See page 26 of the Old Town Walk chapter.

▲Havelská Market

Open-air marketplace. While it's dominated by produce on weekdays, you'll find more souvenirs, puppets, and toys on weekends.

✪ See page 34 of the Old Town Walk chapter.

▲Klementinum

The Czech Republic's massive National Library borders touristy Karlova street. The contrast could not be starker: Step out of the most souvenir-packed stretch of Eastern Europe, and enter the meditative silence of Eastern Europe's biggest library.

Jesuits built the Klementinum in the 1600s to house a new college to offset the influence of the predominantly Protestant Charles University nearby. The building became a library in the early 1700s, and formed the

The Klementinum has a fine Baroque library.

Charles Bridge—atmospheric by night or day

nucleus of today's National and University Library—six million volumes strong.

A few parts of the complex are open to the public, by tour only (45 minutes, in English). You'll see the ornate Baroque Hall—a library with its many centuries-old books. On the fancy ceilings are Jesuit leaders and saints overseeing the pursuit of knowledge, and Josef II—the enlightened Habsburg emperor—looking on from the far end. Then you'll climb the Observatory Tower, learning how early astronomers charted the skies over Prague. The tour finishes with a grand Prague view from the top.

▶ *Tour—220 Kč, departs daily every half-hour 10:00-17:30; shorter hours off-season, tel. 221-663-165, mobile 603-231-241, www.klementinum. com; strolling down Karlova, turn at the intersection with Liliová through an archway into the Klementinum's courtyard.*

▲▲▲Charles Bridge (Karlův Most)

Prague's landmark icon—connecting the two halves of the city across the Vltava River, and lined with statues of Czech saints—is one of Europe's most famous bridges, and one of its best public spaces. Day and night, the bridge bustles with buskers, tourists, street vendors, school groups, impromptu concerts...and, occasionally, a few Czechs.

✪ See the Old Town Walk chapter.

You can climb the **bridge towers** on both ends of the Charles Bridge for equally stunning views. The tower on the **Old Town side** of the river (Staroměstská Mostecká Věž, 138 steps) has the best lighting early in the day. On the **Little Quarter side** (Malostranská Mostecká Věž, 146 step), the best lighting is late in the day.

▶ *Tower climbs each cost 90 Kč, April-Sept daily 10:00-22:00, March and Oct until 20:00, Nov-Feb until 18:00.*

▲▲▲Jewish Quarter (Josefov)

The Jewish Quarter is Europe's most accessible sight for learning about an important culture and faith that's interwoven with the fabric of Central and Eastern Europe. Within a three-block radius, several original synagogues, cemeteries, and other landmarks survive. Today most are collected into one big, well-presented museum—the Jewish Museum in Prague, covered with a single ticket.

> ✪ See the Jewish Quarter Tour chapter.

▲▲Museum of Medieval Art at St. Agnes Convent (Středověké umění v Čechách a Střední Evropě)

This is two sights in one: a collection of graceful religious art from Prague's Golden Age (14th century), housed in a historic building. The second-floor museum traces the evolution of Central European art from 1200 to 1500. It's surprisingly cosmopolitan, combining Czech folk art with Italian poses, French love of nature, and Byzantine gold-leaf backgrounds.

Room A—Aspects of Mary: The mother of Jesus was adored in medieval Europe. You'll see statues and paintings of her smiling, sitting, standing, thoughtful, playful, majestic, with or without a crown, cradling her baby or on her own. These first works date from the 1200s, when this building was a world of women—the convent of St. Agnes.

Room B—Vyssi Brod paintings: These gold-backed paintings tell the story of Christ in a crude medieval style. In the *Annunciation,* the angel literally announces (you can actually read his words) "Ave gratia plena...."

Museum of Medieval Art has many Marys…

…and Charlemagne, forerunner of Czech kings.

Exploring the St. Agnes Convent

In 1233, Prague's Princess Agnes, the daughter of the Czech king, met a famous Italian nun—Clare, a friend of the charismatic St. Francis of Assisi. Agnes established a branch of the Poor Clare nuns here in Prague. She built this complex, consisting of a convent, churches, and the city's first hospital—all of it state-of-the-art.

The Cloister: The heart of the complex is an open-air courtyard surrounded by a covered arcade—that is, a cloister. You can wander through the (mostly empty) rooms surrounding the courtyard, and imagine how the nuns once lived, secluded from the outside world. In the refectory they ate meals, copied manuscripts, and prayed many times a day. The convent was also the first hospital in Prague, known for their secret healing elixir, called "swallow water."

The Church of the Salvator—the former Premyslid crypt: The convent's church became the official burial place for the ruling family of Bohemia, the Premyslids. On the floor, find two burial plaques: Queen Kunigund (d. 1248), the granddaughter of the great Frederick I Barbarossa, and her husband King Wenceslas I, who saved Bohemia from the Mongol hordes of Genghis Khan.

Agnes' Oratory: This humble room is where Agnes Premyslid—the brainy daughter of the king, and one of the most sought-after women in Europe—spent her days. She rejected her many powerful suitors to become a bride of Christ and Mother Superior to this convent. When Agnes died, some speculate that she was buried here. A legend says that whenever her remains are found, the Czech nation will enter a new Golden Age. Her feast day on November 26 coincided with the Velvet Revolution, so Agnes is regarded as the patron saint of Czech democracy, and she graces the 50-Kč bill.

In the *Nativity,* Mary gives birth in a crudely drawn shack. Still, the artist is experimenting with Italian-style 3-D—there's a definite foreground (the couple with water basin) and background (grazing animals).

Room C—Master Theodoricus: During Prague's Golden Age (c. 1350), Emperor Charles IV hired Theodoric of Prague—the country's first "name" artist. Theodoric's saints are real people. They're massive, filling the frames, as if peering out windows. *Charlemagne,* the first Holy Roman Emperor, holds the same coronation objects used by Prague's kings: the golden scepter, orb, and shield with the double-headed eagle. He sports Master Theodoric's signature style: the beard, the thick outlines, brilliant colors, and "soft-focus" features.

Rooms G, H—The "Beautiful Style": These Madonna statues are deliberately graceful, with delicate, curved lines. Mary smiles sweetly, her body sways seductively, her deeply creased robe is luxuriant, and Jesus squirms playfully in her arms. Worshippers were treated to these happy, once colorfully painted, and "beautiful" images of an inviting saint—a vision of how the worlds of the spirit and flesh could unite harmoniously.

The Large Hall (Rooms J, K, L)—Foreign Influence: The harmony of the Czech Golden Age was shattered in the 1400s by religious warfare. The Czech lands and its art were soon dominated by foreigners—as displayed in this large hall. There's some glorious stuff here (*St. George Altar,* the *Puchner Ark*), but it lacks the distinctive look of native Bohemian art. Room M has some of Albrecht Durer's fascinating Apocalypse woodcuts.

From the Large Hall, a staircase leads down to the "churches"—that is, the convent buildings (see sidebar).

Museum-150 Kč*, convent buildings are free, Tue-Sun 10:00-18:00, closed Mon, two blocks northeast of Spanish Synagogue, along the river at Anežská 12, tel. 224-810-628, www.ngprague.cz.*

THE NEW TOWN (NOVÉ MĚSTO)

Enough of pretty, medieval Prague—let's leap into the modern era. The New Town, with Wenceslas Square as its focal point, is today's urban Prague. As you cross Na Příkopě street, you leave the winding lanes and souvenir shops behind, and enter a town of bustling boulevards and fancy malls. The New Town also has remarkable Art Nouveau architecture and reminders of Prague's communist-era past.

▲▲Wenceslas Square (Václavské Náměstí)

More a long, broad boulevard than a square, this city landmark is named for St. Wenceslas, whose equestrian statue overlooks the square's top end. As a popular gathering place, Wenceslas Square has functioned as a stage for modern Czech history.

✪ See the Wenceslas Square Walk chapter.

▲▲Mucha Museum (Muchovo Museum)

This enjoyable little museum features a small selection of the insistently likeable art of Alfons Mucha (MOO-kah, 1860-1939), a founding father of the Art Nouveau movement. It's all crammed into a too-small space, some of the art is faded, and the admission price is steep, but there's no better place to see the posters that made Mucha famous. (For a good general bio of Mucha, see page 96.)

Section 1: Start with the timeline with photos showing Mucha, his wife Maruska, and some of the luminaries they hung out with, like Paul Gauguin and composer Leos Janacek. Next up are Mucha's signature works: posters of willowy maidens—with flowing hair and gowns, curvaceous poses, and flowers in their hair—representing the Four Seasons, Four Arts, and Four Times of Day. The ladies intertwine in the foliage around them, framed by Tiffany-glass backdrops and radiating pastel tones.

Section 2: Mucha burst onto the scene in 1894 with a single poster, advertising a play starring the French actress Sarah Bernhardt as Gismonda. When Parisians started stealing the posters for themselves, it was clear Mucha was on to something. The posters are lithographs, a printing process popularized in Paris (think Toulouse-Lautrec's ads for

The Mucha Museum tells of the man…

…and his willowy Art Nouveau style.

can-can shows). The artist draws on a stone slab with a grease crayon, then coats the slab with water. The ink sticks to the greasy areas and is repelled by the watery parts. It was easy to crank out cheap four-color posters—intended as throwaway advertising but soon accepted as high art.

Sections 3 and 4: On the left wall, find *Documents Decoratifs,* Mucha's how-to manual for Art Nouveau. On the right wall are more posters, but now with Czech themes. Now home from Paris, Mucha got caught up in Czech patriotism. The fragile Parisian maidens become stout Czech peasants and strong workers. Also, see the much-reproduced *Princess Hyacinth*—reclining in a chair with a frank, unflinching gaze.

Sections 5, 6, and 7: Viewing Mucha's paintings, remember that paint was not his main medium. His drawings and pastels (and sketchbooks on the left wall) give a glimpse at how he turned small-scale motifs into larger masterworks. The museum displays some personal elements: photos he took in his Paris studio, an easel painting of his kids, and his desk and chair.

Video: The 30-minute video is a good once-over of his life, and sets the stage for Mucha's masterpiece—the *Slav Epic* (in Prague's Veletržní Palace).

▶ *240 Kč, daily 10:00-18:00, good English descriptions, well-stocked gift shop, two blocks off of Wenceslas Square at Panská 7, tel. 224-233-355, www.mucha.cz.*

▲Museum of Communism (Muzeum Komunismu)

This small museum traces the story of communism in Prague: the origin, dream, reality, and nightmare; the cult of personality; the 40 years of Soviet politics "in all its dreariness and puffed-up glory"; and, finally, the Velvet Revolution—all thoughtfully described in English. The one-way, chronological route tells this story:

It's 1918. World War I ends, and Czechoslovakia is born. But it's weak and divided and easily overrun by Adolf Hitler in World War II.

At war's end, the "Liberation of Prague" was courtesy of the Russian Soviets. They install a communist regime and isolate the Czechs from the West. Soon Prague is speckled with huge statues of communist heroes Lenin and Marx, and a 50-foot stone monstrosity of Soviet dictator Josef Stalin that overlooked the entire city. (Continue around the corner into the next set of rooms.)

Daily life under communism was bleak: empty store shelves, forcibly collectivized farms, sporting events treated like Cold War battlefields...all the while, the focus is on heavy industry (steelworks) and weapons (guns, tanks, uranium). Propaganda posters pacified the masses, showing sturdy, heroic workers and soldiers battling the evils of capitalism. (Continue to the corner rooms.)

The museum reconstructs an interrogation office. The communist government spied on its own people. Your building janitor, your favorite bartender, even your own family members might be secretly reporting your movements to the authorities. Dissidents were arrested, interrogated, tortured, and sent (see the map) to a system of prison camps. Resistance was futile. (Or was it? Turn the corner...)

In 1968, the Prague Spring showed that freedom fighters would not give up. Jan Palach burned himself in protest. Playwright Vaclav Havel endured a prison sentence. And underground rock bands like The Plastic People of the Universe pushed back.

Finally, the museum has a small-scale reproduction of the greatest symbol of communist oppression—the Berlin Wall. When the Wall came

The Museum of Communism illustrates Soviet oppression: This is a copy of the Berlin Wall.

down in Germany in October 1989, the rest of the Soviet empire fell like dominoes. In November 1989, 300,000 Czechs gathered in Wenceslas Square to demand that the Soviets leave—a peaceful movement called the Velvet Revolution. Freedom! As a visitor, you feel it when you escape through a hole in the Wall.

▶ *190 Kč, daily 9:00-21:00, Na Příkopě 10, tel. 224-212-966, www.muzeum komunismu.cz.*

▲▲Municipal House (Obecní Dům)

This Art Nouveau masterpiece (built 1905-1911) is impressive from the outside, but its highlight is the interior—and it's free.

For a description of the building's exterior, ✪ see page 29 in the Old Town Walk chapter.

The Interior: Don't be timid about poking around the interior, which is open to the public. Enter under the green, wrought-iron arcade. In the **rotunda,** admire the mosaic floor, stained glass, the woodwork doorway and the lighting fixtures. To the left is the **café** *(kavárna),* a harmony of woodwork, marble, metal, and glittering chandeliers. Having lunch or a drink here (150-Kč sandwiches, 250-Kč salads, and 200 Kč for coffee and apple strudel) is a great way to experience the decor, but you can also just glimpse it from the doorway (as you "check out the menu"). Opposite the café is the equally stunning **restaurant.**

From the rotunda, step into the **lobby,** where you can gaze up the grand staircase (no tourist access upstairs). The box office sells tickets for concerts, and for the building's temporary exhibits.

Go right and head **downstairs.** Admire the colorful tiles in the stairwell and in the downstairs main room. Check out the **American Bar**

The Municipal House's rich rooms…

…include a (reasonably priced) café.

(salute the US flags above the bar) and the **Plzeňská Restaurant** (with its dark-wood booths and colorful tile scenes of happy peasants).

Finish your tour back upstairs at the **Modernista gift shop** (tucked behind the grand staircase), full of fancy teacups and jewelry.

▶ *Public spaces are free, open daily 10:00-18:00. Daily one-hour English tours take you through other sumptuous areas (290 Kč, usually 3/ day, leaving between 11:00 and 17:00; tours often fill up, buy tickets at ground-floor shop). Concerts are held regularly in the lavish Smetana Hall (see www.obecnidum.cz/web/en/programme). Located at Náměstí Republiky 5, tel. 222-002-101, www.obecnidum.cz.*

▲Powder Tower

Former city gate adorned with 500-year-old Gothic statues. ✪ See page 29 in the Old Town Walk chapter.

▲ The Vltava River—Boats and Beaches

Hour-long Vltava River **boat cruises** leave from near the castle end of the Charles Bridge about hourly. They're scenic and relaxing, but you might spend half the time waiting to go through the locks, and the commentary is mediocre (150-200 Kč).

You can **rent a rowboat or paddleboat** on the island called Střelecký Ostrov, in the middle of the Bridge of Legions (Most Legií), south of the Charles Bridge. You'll float among the swans, surrounded by Prague's architectural splendor (40 Kč/hour for rowboats, 60 Kč/hour for paddleboats, bring photo ID for deposit).

Prague's **best beaches** for swimming (bring your swimsuit) are on the north tip of the island called Střelecký Ostrov.

The Vltava River—row, swim…

…or take a slow and scenic cruise.

▲▲Tram #22—Welcome to Prague Self-Guided Tram Tour

Tram #22—from the New Town to Prague Castle—makes a good orientation joyride and a handy way to reach the castle (see route marked in blue on map on pages 4-5). It runs every 5-10 minutes, and you can hop on and off as you like (32-Kč standard ticket valid for 1.5 hours—for more on riding the trams, see page 168). At any stop, you can get off and catch a Tram #22 going the opposite direction to return to town. Be warned: Thieves and plainclothes ticket-checkers like this route as much as tourists.

Start at the **Národní Třída** stop (there's also a Metro stop here). Catch Tram #22 on the same side of Spálená street as the Tesco department store. Let's go!

At the first stop, **Národní Divadlo,** you'll see the National Theater. Then you cross the Vltava River with its islands, beaches and boat-rental wharves.

Once across the river, the **Újezd** stop faces a park, with the bronze Monument to Victims of Communism and a funicular that leads to the Eiffel-like Petřín Tower.

The tram then heads north from the **Hellichova** stop. On the right is Kampa Island (fun to stroll). On the left, the tram passes St. Mary the Victorious Church, popular with pilgrims for its Infant Jesus of Prague. As the tram gradually goes uphill, you're entering the Little Quarter.

At **Malostranské Náměstí** (closest stop to the Charles Bridge), you're in Little Quarter Square, the neighborhood's focal point, dominated by the Church of St. Nicholas. From here you can hike up Nerudova street to Prague Castle.

(Note that a major overhaul of the tram system may affect the route at this point, so let's skip ahead a few stops to the next major stop—Malostranská.)

At the **Malostranská** stop, on the left is the entry to the Wallenstein Palace Garden. Behind you, on the right in the park, is a modern memorial to WWII freedom fighters. The tram now starts a long climb up the hill.

The next stop is **Královský Letohrádek.** Immediately across the street is the Royal Summer Palace, the Royal Gardens leading fragrantly to Prague Castle.

Get ready: The next stop, **Pražský Hrad,** is the most direct route to the castle entrance. Or stay on board for my favorite approach to the castle—from Pohořelec, coming up soon.

At **Brusnice** you could explore the Nový Svět (New World)

neighborhood, a time capsule of cobblestone streets and tiny houses with no shops or tourists. The tram now winds through a greenbelt built along the remains of the city wall.

Finally, you reach the end of our tour—**Pohořelec.** Here is the Strahov Monastery (see page 133). From here, you could visit the monastery, then stroll 10 minutes downhill to the castle. Or catch a tram going the opposite direction to do this trip in reverse.

▲National Memorial to the Heroes of the Heydrich Terror (Národní Památník Hrdinů Heydrichiády)

This World War II-era memorial, located in the crypt of the Sts. Cyril and Methodius Church, honors the Czech resistance movement against Nazi oppression.

It's 1942, and the Czech lands are under the thumb of German occupation. The Nazi commander was the hated Reinhard Heydrich—one of Hitler's closest cronies, second-in-command in the SS, organizer of Jewish pogroms, and one of the main architects of the Holocaust. When Heydrich took over Bohemian lands, resistance seemed futile.

But two Czech paratroopers—Jozef Gabčík and Jan Kubiš—signed up for a potentially suicidal mission to take down Heydrich. On the morning of May 27, the two men ambushed Heydrich in his car, in northern Prague. Gabčík fired first, but the gun jammed. Kubiš threw a handmade grenade that wounded Heydrich enough that he died days later. Hitler was outraged and ordered vengeance. Two Czech villages were summarily razed to the ground, and 5,000 were executed. Gabčík and Jan Kubiš fled with a price on their heads and found refuge here in this Greek Orthodox Church. Eventually they were ratted on. On June 18, at 4:15 in the morning, the

Busts of the heroes of the Heydrich Terror

Dancing House, by the American Frank Gehry

Gestapo stormed in, and a two-hour battle ensued. Kubiš was gunned down in the nave of the church. Gabčík committed suicide in the crypt.

Today, a modest exhibition in the crypt retells the story of Czech resistance. Back outside, notice the small memorial, including bullet holes, plaque, and flowers on the street.

▶ *The memorial entrance is around the corner from the front of the church. 75 Kč, good 25-Kč booklet, Tue-Sun 9:00-17:00, closed Mon, at Resslova 9A, tel. 224-916-100. The* **Dancing House,** *a whimsical modern building by architect Frank Gehry, is 2 blocks west of the Heydrich memorial at Jiráskovo náměstí 1981.*

THE LITTLE QUARTER (MALÁ STRANA)

Huddled under the castle on the west bank of the river, this neighborhood is pleasant, though low on blockbuster sights. The Little Quarter was one of the original four towns that comprised old Prague. After the original merchant settlement burned down in the 1540s, it rose from the ashes to become a Baroque town of fine palaces and gardens. The most enjoyable approach from the Old Town is across the Charles Bridge and straight up Mostecká street to the Little Quarter Square (Malostranské Náměstí) with its huge Church of St. Nicholas.

Little Quarter Square (Malostranské Náměstí) and Church of St. Nicholas (Kostel Sv. Mikuláše)

The focal point of this neighborhood is split into an upper and lower part by the domineering Church of St. Nicholas and its adjacent Jesuit college. The square has a Baroque plague column and a handy Via Musica ticket office. Nerudova Street—a steep, cobbled, atmospheric lane—leads from the square up to the castle.

This church, not to be confused with the larger Church of St. Nicholas on the Old Town Square, is Prague's best example of High Baroque (built 1703-1760). The interior is giddy with curves and illusions, all under a vision-of-heaven dome. In the left transept, stairs lead to several large paintings by Karel Škréta, the greatest Czech Baroque painter. You can climb 215 steps up the bell tower for a good look at the city and the church's 250-foot dome.

▶ *Church: 70 Kč, daily 9:00-17:00, until 16:00 Nov-Feb, opens at 8:30 for prayer. Tower: 90 Kč, daily April-Oct 10:00-22:00, shorter hours in winter, tower entrance is outside the right transept (www.stnicholas.cz).*

Sights near Little Quarter Square

Two sights lie between Little Quarter Square and the Charles Bridge: The **Lennon Wall** (Lennonova Zeď)—named for rock singer John Lennon—is covered with colorful graffiti. Since 1980, the wall has been a symbol of free expression. While the ideas of V. I. Lenin collapsed in 1989, the hopeful message of J. W. Lennon lives on. **Kampa Island** is a colorful neighborhood of relaxing pubs, a breezy park, hippies, lovers, a fine contemporary art gallery, and river access.

A 10-minute walk north of the Square (near the Malostranská Metro station) is the entrance to the **Wallenstein Palace Garden** (Valdštejnská Palac Zahrada). Of the neighborhood's many impressive palace gardens open to the public, this is by far the largest and most beautiful, with a large pool, Greek-style statues, amphitheater, and fake grotto (free, April-Oct Mon-Fri 7:30-18:00, Sat-Sun 10:00-18:00, June-Sept daily until 19:00; closed Nov-March).

A 5-minute walk south of the Square is the **Church of St. Mary the Victorious** (Kostel Panny Marie Vítězné), which displays the small statue of the Infant of Prague. Christians from across the globe (especially South America) make the pilgrimage to Prague just to kneel before this humble baby (free, Mon-Sat 9:30-17:30, Sun 13:00-18:00, Karmelitská 9, www.pragjesu.info).

Kampa Island's easygoing rustic ambience

Wallenstein Palace Garden's elegance

Petřín Hill, reached by a funicular, boasts a mini Eiffel Tower and great city views.

▲**Petřín Hill (Petřínské Sady)**

This hill, accessed by a funicular at the south end of the Little Quarter, features several unusual sights.

At the base of the hill (near the intersection of Újezd and Vítězná streets) stands the **Monument to Victims of Communism** (Pomník Obětem Komunismu). The statues—representing the victims of the totalitarian regime—gradually atrophy as they disappear up the hillside steps. The statistics inscribed on the steps say it all: From 1948 until 1989, in Czechoslovakia alone, 205,486 people were imprisoned, 248 were executed, 4,500 died in prison, 327 were shot attempting to cross the border, and 170,938 left the country.

To the left of the monument is the **Hunger Wall** (Hladová Zed'). This medieval defense wall was built by Prague's poor in the days of Charles IV (14th century) as a work-for-food project.

To the right of the Monument to Victims of Communism (50 yards away) is the **funicular** up Petřín Hill—hop on to reach Petřín Tower (uses tram/Metro ticket, runs daily every 10-15 minutes 8:00-22:00).

At the summit of the hill stands an Eiffel Tower look-alike—the **Petřín Tower.** Built for an exhibition in 1891, the 200-foot-tall Petřín Tower is one-fifth the height of its Parisian big brother, built two years earlier. But, thanks to this hill, the top of the tower sits at the same elevation as the real Eiffel Tower. Climbing the 400 steps (105 Kč, daily 10:00-22:00, shorter hours off-season) rewards you with amazing views of the city. Czech wives drag their men to Petřín Hill each May Day to reaffirm their love with a kiss under a blooming sour-cherry tree.

THE CASTLE QUARTER (HRADČANY)

Looming above Prague, dominating its skyline, is the Castle Quarter. Prague Castle and its surrounding sights are packed with Czech history, as well as tourists. To get there, you can walk (20 minutes uphill from the Charles Bridge), take a taxi, or ride the tram. Visit the castle early or late to minimize crowds. For detailed information on transportation options and castle strategies, see page 76.

▲▲**Prague Castle (Pražský Hrad)**

This vast and sprawling complex has been the seat of Czech power for centuries. It has a wide range of sights and museums within its walls, including the vital St. Vitus Cathedral, its former royal palace, a higgledy-piggledy lane, and an assortment of history and art museums. The castle's official sights share the same opening hours and tickets.

All of the details are covered in ☼ the Prague Castle Tour chapter.

▲▲▲St. Vitus Cathedral (Katedrála Sv. Víta)

Rising from the center of the castle complex is this towering house of worship. It sports flying buttresses and spiny spires outside and stained glass by Mucha inside. St. Vitus is the top church of the Czech people. Many VIPs from this nation's history—from saints to statesmen—are buried here, including the most important Czech saint, St. Wenceslas.

For a self-guided tour of the cathedral, ☼ see the Prague Castle Tour chapter.

▲▲Lobkowicz Palace (Lobkowiczký Palác)

This palace, at the bottom of the castle complex, displays the private collection of a prominent Czech noble family, including paintings, ceramics, and musical scores. The Lobkowiczes' property was confiscated by the communists in 1948. In 1990, William Lobkowicz, then a Boston investment banker, returned to Czechoslovakia, reclaimed his family's property, and opened his palace to the public.

Visiting the Palace: A conscientious host, William Lobkowicz himself narrates the delightful, included audioguide. Use the map that comes with your ticket to hone in on the highlights:

The Second-Floor Landing and Room B: As you pass by the portraits of Lobkowicz's ancestors, listen to their stories, including that of Polyxena, whose determination saved two Catholic governors defenestrated next door (by hiding them under her skirt).

Room G: The family loved music. See their instruments, including old lutes. There's the manuscript of Beethoven's *Eroica* symphony (with his last-minute changes). The piece was dedicated to his sponsor—Prince Lobkowicz (see his portrait)—and premiered at the Lobkowicz Palace in Vienna. Nearby is Mozart's handwritten reorchestration of Handel's *Messiah.*

Rooms H-J: The highlights of the museum's paintings include Pieter Bruegel the Elder's magnificently preserved *Haymaking,* from 1565. It's one of the earliest entirely secular landscape paintings in Europe (showing an idyllic connection between peasants and nature). Admire a few paintings of various Lobkowicz castles (by no-name artists), as well as two Canaletto scenes of London's Westminster Abbey and St. Paul's Cathedral.

▶ *275 Kč, includes audioguide, daily 10:00-18:00, last entry one hour before closing, tel. 233-312-925, www.lobkowicz.cz. Café with view. The charming young man you may see selling ice cream out front is William's son, Will.*

▲Strahov Monastery and Library (Strahovský Klášter a Knihovna)

The Strahov Monastery, with its landmark domes, sits above the castle. If you'd like to combine the monastery with your castle visit, it's easy to ride Tram #22 up to the Pohořelec stop (beyond the castle), visit the monastery,

The Strahov Monastery library has a painted ceiling and a locked case of (once) prohibited books.

then walk 10 minutes down to Castle Square—passing Loreta Church on the way.

In its heyday, Strahov Monastery was bustling with monks creating a booming economy of its own, with vineyards, a brewery, and a sizeable beer hall—all open once again.

The **main church** was decorated by the monks in textbook Baroque (usually closed, but peek through the doors). Go ahead, inhale. That's the scent of Baroque.

The **library** offers a peek at enlightened thinkers of the 18th century. The big philosophy room (seen only from the doors) is filled with 10th- to 17th-century books, shelved under elaborately painted ceilings. A second hall—down a hallway lined with antique furniture—focuses on theology. At the far end of this room, notice the gilded, locked case containing the *libri prohibiti*—prohibited books. Only the abbot had the key.

Back outside, find the **Klášterní Pivovar beerhall,** where they brew beer just as monks have for centuries (daily 10:00-22:00, also serves meals). Don't miss the monastery's **garden terrace** with exquisite views over the domes and spires of Prague; the **Bellavista Restaurant** here is a good value if the weather's clear (daily 11:00-24:00).

If you stroll down to the castle, you'll pass the **Museum of Miniatures** (Muzeum Miniatur), whose 40 teeny exhibits could all fit in a carry-on-size suitcase (100 Kč, kids-50 Kč, daily 9:00-17:00, Strahovské Nádvoří 11). Then you'll pass Loreta Church (described next).

▶ *Strahov Monastery grounds are free and always open; library—80 Kč, an extra 50 Kč to take photos—strictly enforced; daily 9:00-11:45 & 13:00-17:00, last entry 15 minutes earlier, www.strahovskyklaster.cz. (A pay WC is just to the right of the monastery entrance.)*

Loreta Church

This church is a hit with pilgrims for its dazzling bell tower, garden-like cloister, sparkling treasury, and much-venerated Holy House.

In the cloister stands the ornate **Santa Casa (Holy House),** thought to be part of Mary's home in Nazareth, with an original beam. It's a ho-hum tourist sight, but believers consider this the holiest spot in the country.

The small **Baroque church** is one of the most beautiful in Prague—though the rich marble-and-gold décor is all fake. In the cloister's final corner is **"St. Bearded Woman"** (Svatá Starosta). This pious woman escaped a bad marriage by miraculously sprouting a beard...and the guy said, "No way." Hordes of sympathetic worshippers light candles here to this patron saint of unhappy marriages.

Upstairs in the bank-vault-like **treasury** is a monstrance (Communion wafer holder) from 1699, with more than 6,000 diamonds. Enjoy the short **carillon concert** at the top of the hour.

▶ *130 Kč, daily April-Oct 9:00-12:15 & 13:00-17:00, Nov-March 9:30-12:15 & 13:00-16:00, audioguide-150 Kč, tel. 220-516-740, www.loreta.cz.*

SIGHTS OUTSIDE THE CENTER

▲▲▲Alfons Mucha's *Slav Epic*
Mucha created a wide variety of Art Nouveau illustrations throughout his illustrious career. But his magnum opus is this series of 20 thrilling, movie-screen-sized canvases telling the epic story of the Slavic people.

✪ See the *Slav Epic* Tour chapter.

▲Vyšehrad
If you're looking to escape the tourists—while digging more deeply into Czech culture and history (and also enjoying fine city views)—head for the

A short Metro ride from the center gets you to a park with a patriotic history.

hilltop fortress-turned-park called Vyšehrad (VEE-sheh-rahd), just south of the center. While there, ogle the dynamic statues of Bohemian folkloric figures and dip into the National Cemetery to pay your respects to Czech greats such as Mucha and Dvořák.

The park is free to enter and open all the time (though the church closes at 18:00 and the cemetery closes as early as 17:00 off-season). To get there, ride the Metro to the Vyšehrad stop and hike five minutes downhill.

▲▲Day Trips from Prague

The Czech Republic offers a wide range of interesting one-day side-trips. Kutná Hora is a workaday Czech town with an offbeat bone church, stunning cathedral, and silver mining museum. Terezín was the notorious Theresienstadt Nazi concentration camp, now a sobering memorial. Three castles compete for your attention: Konopiště Castle is the opulent but lived-in former residence of the Archduke Franz Ferdinand. Karlštejn Castle is historic and dramatically situated. Křivoklát Castle is a genuinely Gothic hunting palace. And Karlovy Vary (Carlsbad) is a well-known and swanky spa town.

You could do these on your own by public transportation or a rental car—but that's beyond the scope of this city guide. Several bus companies offer guided day trips: Try Premiant City Tours (www.premiant.cz) or Wittmann Tours (www.wittmann-tours.com). Or consider Mike's Chauffeur Service (page 170), Magic Praha (page 168), or a private guide (page 180).

Sleeping

I've grouped my hotel listings into four neighborhoods: the **Old Town** (central and atmospheric but more expensive), the **Little Quarter** (quiet and quaint, walking distance to Old Town and castle), **Beyond Wenceslas Square** (better value, less-touristed, walk or short tram ride to center), and **Farther from the Center** (best value, 15-minute tram ride to center).

I like hotels that are clean, central, good-value, friendly, run with a respect for Czech traditions, and small enough to have a hands-on owner and stable staff. Four of these six virtues means it's a keeper. Double rooms listed in this book average around 3,000 Kč (including a private bathroom). I've also included several pensions (bed-and-breakfasts) and hostels (beds in a dorm room and a few doubles).

Book as far in advance as possible, especially for May, June, September, Easter, and New Year's.

Sleep Code

$$$ Higher Priced—Most rooms 3,500 Kč or more
$$ Moderately Priced—Most rooms 2,500-3,500 Kč
$ Lower Priced—Most rooms 2,500 Kč or less

These rates are for a standard double room with bath during high season. Unless otherwise noted, credit cards are accepted, breakfast and tax are included, English is spoken, and Wi-Fi is generally free. Prices change; verify current rates online or by email. For the best prices, always book directly with the hotel.

A Typical Prague Hotel Room

A typical 3,000 Kč double room in Prague will be small by American standards. It will have one double bed (either queen-sized or slightly narrower) or two twins. There's probably a bathroom in the room with a toilet, sink, and bathtub or shower. The room has a telephone and TV, and may have a safe. Single rooms, triples, and quads will have similar features.

Many of my listings are in old townhouses—charming, but they might be somewhat creaky, have very steep stairs, and no elevator.

Breakfast—often included in the room price—is normally a self-service buffet of fresh bread, cereal, ham, cheese, yogurt, juice, and coffee or tea.

The hotel will have Internet access, either Wi-Fi or a public terminal in the lobby. At many of my listings, at least one of these options is free. The staff speaks English.

Making Reservations

Make reservations by phone, through the hotel's website, or with an email that reads something like this:

Dear Hotel Prague,
I would like to reserve a double room for 2 people for 3 nights, arriving 19 July and departing 22 July. If possible, I would like a quiet room with a double bed (not twin beds), a view of the river, and a shower (not a tub). Please let me know if you have a room available and the price. Thank you.

If they require your credit-card number for a deposit, you can send it by email (I do), but it's safer via phone, the hotel's secure website, or split between two emails. Once your room is booked, print out the confirmation, and reconfirm your reservation with a phone call or email a day or two in advance (alert them if you'll be arriving after 17:00). If canceling a reservation, some hotels require advance notice—otherwise they may bill you. Even if there's no penalty, it's polite to give at least three days' notice.

Budget Tips

To get the best rates, book directly with the hotel, not through a hotel-booking engine. Start with the hotel's website, looking for promo deals. (Most rack rates—the standard full price—are given in euros, so my listed prices in crowns may differ somewhat due to currency fluctuations.) Check rates every few days, as prices can vary greatly based on demand. Email several hotels to ask for their best price and compare offers—you may be astonished at the range.

You'll find the best deals traveling in July or August (rates generally 15 percent lower) and from November through March (30 percent lower). Despite what the online rack rate says, it's often possible to negotiate a discount by email or in person. Some places may give a discount if you stay at least three nights or pay in cash. Some of my listings offer a "Rick Steves discount" if you book directly, ask in advance, and show this book when you check in.

Besides hotels, there are cheaper alternatives. Pensions (the local word for bed-and-breakfasts) offer a personal touch at a fair price—I've listed several. I also list a few all-ages hostels, which offer cheap dorm beds (400 Kč) and a few inexpensive doubles (1,200 Kč), and come with curfews and other rules. Airbnb.com makes it reasonably easy to find a place to sleep in someone's home.

If you can handle the uncertainty and hassle (many can't), you can save about 30 percent by showing up without a reservation and finding accommodations upon arrival. Prague is awash with overpriced hotel rooms on the push list, private rooms for rent, booking services at the train station, and roving entrepreneurs looking to rent you a room in a hotel or private apartment. With a little effort, you can almost always find a reasonable room, though it may not be your ideal choice.

Consider a local room-booking service: The Athos Travel website offers everything from hostels to five-star hotels, mainly in the Old Town (tel. 241-440-571, www.a-prague.com; strictly-enforced cancellation fees). Touristpoint, both online (www.touristpoint.cz) and on site at the Main Train Station (daily 8:00-22:00, tel. 224-946-010), has a slew of moderately priced hotels and pensions (but be clear on the location, as some are far from the center). Lída Jánská's Magic Praha can book accommodations, including a nice apartment near the Jewish Quarter (mobile 604-207-225, www.magicpraha.cz).

Renting an apartment can save money if you're traveling as a family, staying more than a week, and planning to cook your own meals. Try homeaway.com (offering a wide range of listings) or vrbo.com (putting you directly in touch with owners).

Don't be too cheap when picking a place to stay. Anything under 2,500 Kč (even my listings) can be a little rough around the edges. Choose a nice, central neighborhood. In the rowdy tourist zone or on a busy boulevard, consider asking for a quiet room in back. Your Prague experience will be more memorable with a welcoming oasis to call home.

OLD TOWN: Sights, restaurants, pubs, and ambience make this area desirable but higher priced. All my listings are within a 10-minute walk of the Old Town Square.	
$$$ Hotel Metamorphosis Malá Štupartská 5 | tel. 221-771-011 www.hotelmetamorphis.cz	Splurge in solidly renovated medieval building, noisy street-side rooms
$$ Hotel Maximilian Haštalská 14 | tel. 225-303-111 www.maximilianhotel.com	Business-class comfort, sleek and mod decor, on quiet hidden square
$$ Brewery Hotel u Medvídků Na Perštýně 7 | tel. 224-211-916 www.umedvidku.cz	Comfortably renovated rooms in dark-wood medieval building with beerhall, ask about Rick Steves discount
$$ Design Hotel Jewel Prague Rytířská 3 | tel. 224-211-699 www.hoteljewelprague.com	Modern comfortable rooms in small plain building near Old Town Square, Rick Steves discount
$ Green Garland Pension Řetězová 10 | tel. 222-220-178 www.uzv.cz	Warm and personal on cobbled lane, clean and simple wood-beam charm, no elevator

$ **Hotel Haštal** Haštalská 16 | tel. 222-314-335 www.hastal.com	Family-run, on quiet hidden square, Rick Steves discount
$ **Old Prague Hostel** Benediktská 2 | tel. 224-829-058 www.oldpraguehostel.com	Dorm beds, some doubles, well-worn rooms, near Powder Tower, indifferent staff, more for young backpackers
$ **Hostel Týn** Týnská 19 | tel. 224-808-301 www.hostelpraguetyn.com	Dorm beds, some doubles, heart of Old Town in quiet courtyard, reserve ahead

LITTLE QUARTER: Quiet, cobbled-lane area near quaint restaurants and shops. Walking distance to castle or Old Town (across the Charles Bridge).

$$$ **Vintage Design Hotel Sax** Jánský Vršek 3 | tel. 257-531-268 www.sax.cz	Stylish retro but modern no-nonsense place, Rick Steves discount
$$$ **Hotel Julián** Elišky Peškové 11, Praha 5 tel. 257-311-150 www.hoteljulian.com	Business-professional, fresh and homey, on south fringe of Little Quarter, Rick Steves discount
$$ **Dům u Velké Boty** Vlašská 30 | tel. 257-532-088 www.bigboot.cz	Quintessential small family-run place, chatty owners, quiet square, cash only, Rick Steves discount

BEYOND WENCESLAS SQUARE: Workaday untouristed urban neighborhoods in New Town, a 10- to 15-minute walk to Wenceslas Square, or easy tram/Metro connections to tourist center.

$$ **Louren Hotel** Slezská 55, Praha 3 | tel. 224-250-025 www.louren.cz	Business-class but small and welcoming, in upscale area, Rick Steves discount
$$ **Hotel 16** Kateřinská 16, Praha 2 tel. 224-920-636 www.hotel16.cz	Small sleek modern business-class, cherry-wood elegance, Rick Steves discount
$ **Hotel Anna** Budečská 17, Praha 2 | tel. 222-513-111 www.hotelanna.cz	Bright simple pastel rooms and basic service

Sleeping

FARTHEST FROM THE CENTER: Do the math: A 10- to 20-minute tram ride can equal a $50-100 savings on a classy hotel room. These areas are quiet and residential, near park-like settings, with easy tram connections, and...far from the center.

$$ Hotel Adalbert Markétská 1, Praha 6 | tel. 220-406-170 www.hoteladalbert.cz	Renovated rooms in working monastery on park-like grounds, join the monks at church or their pub
$$ Hotel u Šemíka Vratislavova 36, Praha 2 tel. 221-965-610 www.usemika.cz	Small place in quiet residential neighborhood, Rick Steves discount
$ Pension Větrník U Větrníku 1, Praha 6 | tel. 220-513-390 www.pensionvetrnik.cz	Former windmill, family-run, offers great food option, airport bus nearby
$ Guest House Lída Lopatecká 26, Praha 4 | tel. 261-214-766 www.lidabb.eu	Friendly family-run, homey spacious rooms, quiet area, has family suite, cash only
$ Sir Toby's Hostel Dělnická 24, Praha 7 | tel. 246-032-610 www.sirtobys.com	Dorm beds, some doubles, clean and friendly, working-class neighborhood
$ Hostel Elf Husitská 11, Praha 3 | tel. 222-540-963 www.hostelelf.com	Dorm beds, some doubles, near Main Train Station, fun-loving and wild, cheap beer

Eating

In Prague you can eat well for less than you'd pay in many European cities. Prague's eateries make for a buffet of dining options. Choose from traditional meat-and-potatoes Czech cuisine in dark-wood restaurants; trendy student-oriented bars; elegant Art Nouveau dining rooms; ethnic and vegetarian eateries; hip modern cafés; or Czech pubs featuring some of the world's best beer.

My listings are in Prague's atmospheric neighborhoods, handy to recommended hotels and sights. Most are in the Old Town, New Town, and Little Quarter. Besides my listings, Prague is an especially good town for wandering the back lanes and discovering your own memorable dining experience. Remember, Prague is two parallel worlds—for tourists and for locals—so make a point of getting off the tourist flow (even a block or two) for better deals, service, and ambience.

Restaurant Price Code

$$$ Most main courses 220 Kč or more
$$ Most main courses 150-220 Kč
$ Most main courses 150 Kč or less

Based on the average price of a main dish on the menu. Salads and appetizers are somewhat cheaper, and many places have deeply discounted lunch specials. A typical dinner at a $$ restaurant—including appetizer, main dish, beer or wine, water, and service—would cost about 400 Kč. (20 Kč = about $1)

My recommended places are varied—some are lunch-only, others are for classy sit-down dinners, some just for a drink or coffee, some takeout delis or grocery stores—so read the descriptions. Be aware that, in this popular city, even my "authentic traditional" places might be pretty touristy. Frankly, most Czechs these days prefer cosmopolitan cuisine to sauerkraut. Still, these traditional places can be a great experience. Expect wonderfully rustic spaces, smoking locals, surly service, and reasonably good, inexpensive food.

When in Prague...

When in Prague, I eat on the Czech schedule. For breakfast, I eat at the hotel (bread, meat, cheese, cereal) or grab a pastry and coffee at a café. Lunch (12:00–14:00) might be a sandwich, ethnic takeout, a light meal in a café, or a restaurant lunch special. In the afternoon, Czechs might enjoy a coffee in an atmospheric café or a beverage with friends at an outdoor table or cozy pub. Dinner (18:00-21:00) is the time for slowing down and savoring a multicourse restaurant meal, or digging into hearty fare in a traditional beerhall.

Restaurants

In general, Prague's restaurants are open Sunday through Thursday 11:00-22:00, and Friday and Saturday 11:00-24:00. Many establishments offer a lunch special 11:00-14:30, called a *hotová jídla*. This is a quick, pre-prepared, ready-to-serve hot meal, including meat and side dishes.

Smoking establishments are the norm—check the sticker on the exterior that indicates whether they allow smoking, prohibit it, or provide a non-smoking section.

Tipping is an issue only at restaurants that have table service. If you're in a place where you order your food at a counter, don't tip. For a sit-down meal at a Czech restaurant that has a waitstaff, the service charge is included in the bill, but it's customary to round up the bill after a good meal (usually 5-10 percent; e.g., for a 370-Kč meal, pay 400 Kč). Overly generous tourists (used to tipping 15 percent or more) have trained Czech waiters to expect American-size tips from their American customers. I still tip on the lower, local end of the scale.

Check the bill carefully to make sure you're not overcharged (a common problem). Understand the expected tip to make sure you don't over-pay: Is the service charge already included (as it should be)? Did the waiter tack on an additional 10 percent service charge above the built-in service charge? If so, then there's no need to "round up" beyond that by tipping the 5 to 10 percent a local might for good service. While many places accept credit cards, I usually pay for meals in cash—it seems to make waiters happier.

Warm up the waiter with a few Czech words—"Hello" (*dobry den;* DOH-bree den), "please" (*prosím;* PROH-zeem) and "thank you" (*děkuji;* DYACK-kwee). You'll get better service and won't be expected to tip more than a local. Believe me: The slightest attempt at speaking Czech (see phrases on page 183) will turn you from a targeted tourist into a special guest, even in the most touristy restaurants. Locals order a beer first, and then, after a sip, ask for the *jídelní lístek* (menu).

A traditional Czech restaurant is a social place where people come to

Lunch specials can be a great deal.

Cafés and pubs also serve meals.

relax. Tables are not necessarily private. You can ask to join someone, and you will most likely make some new friends. Only a rude waiter will rush you. Good service is relaxed (slow to an American). No one will bring you the *účet* (bill) until you ask for it: *"Pane vrchní, zaplatím!"* (PAH-neh VURCH-nee ZAH-plah-teem; "Mr. Waiter, now I pay!").

Cafés, Bars, and Pubs

Besides the full-service restaurant *(restaurace),* you can also generally get food at a pub *(hostinec)* or a bar *(hospoda).* Many cafés also serve light lunches, though some only serve coffee. Prague has plenty of takeout food stands, bakeries (with sandwiches and small pizzas to go), delis with stools or a table, department-store cafeterias, salad bars, and simple little eateries for fast and easy sit-down restaurant food. Wherever you go, a good place to start the experience is by ordering a beer.

Beer (Pivo): Czechs are among the world's most enthusiastic beer drinkers—adults drink an average of 80 gallons a year. The pub is a place to have fun, complain, discuss art and politics, talk hockey, and chat with locals and visitors alike. A beer will land on your table upon the slightest hint to the waiter, and a new pint will automatically appear before the old glass is empty (until you tell the waiter to stop). If you simply order a *pivo,* you'll get a large draft beer (0.5 liter—17 oz); a *malé pivo* is small (0.3 liter—10 oz).

The Czechs invented Pilsner-style lager in nearby Plzeň, and the result, Pilsner Urquell, is on tap in many pubs. Czechs also produce Budvar, from the town of Budějovice—"Budweis" in German. (The Czech company legally owns the name, which is why Anheuser-Busch Budweiser must be sold in the EU under the name of "Bud.") Other Czech beers include

Czechs lo-o-ove beer, especially Pilsners.

Prague offers lots of meals with a view.

Krušovice, Gambrinus, Staropramen, and Kozel. Newer microbrews are gaining in popularity. Most traditional Czech beers are only slightly stronger than typical American brews. (Don't be misled by the double-digit degree symbol on bottles, which indicates density of ingredients, not alcohol content.) Each establishment generally has only one brand of beer on tap. In addition to beer, herb-based liqueurs are popular, chiefly Fernet and Becherovka. When Czechs drink, they don't mix their spirits, or even their brands of beer. For one night, they say, you must stay loyal to one woman and to one beer. *Na zdraví!* "To your health!"

Czech Food

Czech cuisine is heavy on meat, potatoes, and cabbage. It's hearty and tasty—designed to keep peasants fueled through a day of hard work. (For a change of pace, Prague has plenty of ethnic restaurants.)

Starters: Soup *(polévka)* is the essential start of a traditional meal—thick soups for a cold day (cabbage, lentil, or bean), or lighter options (beef or chicken with noodles, leek, cauliflower). Bread *(pečivo)* may be automatically delivered with the soup, or you'll need to ask for it—but either way, you'll be charged for it.

Main Dishes: Roasted meat dishes *(pečené* means roasted) are popular—roast pork, chicken, and duck. Other popular dishes are fried pork fillet *(smažený řízek,* like Wiener schnitzel), goulash stew *(guláš),* and beef tenderloin in cream sauce *(svíčková na smetaně).* Pork knuckle *(vepřové koleno)* is a huge portion to share with friends. In this landlocked country, fish options are less popular. Vegetarians enjoy fried cheese with potatoes *(smažený sýr s bramborem)* and lentils with fried egg *(čočka s vejci).*

Czech cuisine—hearty and fresh

Get dessert to go and stroll the Old Town.

Eating

Side Dishes: You typically order your garnishes separately (except for those meal-on-plate lunch specials). The most common is bread dumplings *(knedlíky)* drowned in gravy. There's also cabbage *(zelím)* and potatoes *(bramborem)*. Your best salad option is probably the Greek-style salad *(sopský salát)*, which is typically eaten with the main dish, unless you tell the waiter to bring it as a starter.

Dessert: Try sweet crepes *(palačinka)*, small pancakes *(lívance)*, a glazed cream puff *(větrník)*, apple strudel, or… more dumplings (filled with fruit). All over Prague's Old Town, you'll find kiosks selling a treat called *trdlo* or *trdelník*—a coil of dough dusted with cinnamon sugar. While these originated in Hungary, they've sort of become "traditional." (Buy them warm, not wrapped in plastic—it makes a big difference.)

Beverages: No Czech meal is complete without the traditional cup of strong *turecká káva*. This is Turkish-style coffee—finely ground coffee that only partly dissolves, leaving "mud" on the bottom, drunk without milk. In restaurants, tap water is generally not served, as Czechs are willing to pay for bottled mineral water. Beer is cheaper.

OLD TOWN: Eateries here are generally more touristy and expensive. My listings are more local and reasonable. If you're browsing on your own, try the Havelská Market (many budget options with views of the market action) or Dlouha Street (running NE of Old Town Square, lined with ethnic food joints). The Old Town Square is overpriced but still unbeatable for nursing a drink or light meal while watching the tide of people.

❶	**$$ Restaurace u Provaznice** Provaznická 3 tel. 224-232-528	All the Czech classics, especially pig leg, amid bawdy frescoes, near bottom of Wenceslas Square
❷	**$$ U Medvídků** Na Perštýně 7 tel. 224-211-916	Big noisy touristy beerhall for Czech Budweiser, a bit smoky
❸	**$ U Zlatého Tygra** Husova 17 tel. 222-221-111	Proverbial Czech pub, usually packed with locals, for beer not food
❹	**$ Jan Paukert** Národní 17 tel. 224-222-615	Century-old deli for open-faced sandwiches *(chlebíčky)* and more
❺	**$$$ Hotel u Prince Terasa** Staroměstské Náměstí 29 tel. 224-213-807	Stunning view terrace over Old Town Square, overpriced and touristy, fun menu or nurse a drink
❻	**$$$ Kolkovna** V Kolkovně 8 tel. 224-819-701	Big woody and modern, fun mix of Czech and international cuisine
❼	**$ Česká Kuchyně** Havelská 23 tel. 224-235-574	Blue-collar, point-to-order cafeteria for super-cheap Czech fare
❽	**$$ Restaurace u Betlémské Kaple** Betlémské Náměstí 2 tel. 222-221-639	Light wooden decor, cheap lunch deals, fish specialties, happy locals
❾	**$$ Restaurace Mlejnice** Kožná 14 tel. 224-228-635	Fun little pub for Czech fare near Old Town Square, reserve for evenings

Eating

⑩	**$ Lokál** Dlouhá 33 tel. 222-316-265	Czech classics, low prices, 1980s retro design, curt waiters, reservations smart
⑪	**$$ Klub Architectu** Betlémské Náměstí 169 tel. 224-248-878	Fun modern dishes and salads, in medieval cellar or outside
⑫	**$$ Indian Jewel** Týn 6 tel. 222-310-156	Excellent Indian cuisine, great outdoor dining experience in historic Ungelt courtyard, lunch specials
⑬	**$$$ Dinitz Kosher Restaurant** Bílkova 12 tel. 222-244-000	Kosher fare in Jewish Quarter, low-key atmosphere, reserve for Shabbat
⑭	**$ Restaurace u Knihovny** Veleslavínova 10 mobile 732-835-876	Traditional Czech fare, friendly, warm interior, popular lunch specials
⑮	**$ Grand Café Orient** Ovocný Trh 19 tel. 224-224-240	Oasis off touristy street inside Cubist House, sandwiches and salads, balcony
⑯	**$ Café Montmartre** Řetězová 7 tel. 222-221-244	Coffee house for poets and thinkers, coffee only (no food), next door is Ebel Coffee House
⑰	**$ James Joyce Irish Pub** U Obecního Dvora 4 tel. 224-818-851	Really? Guinness in Pilsner-mad Prague? Yes, because it's very local
	NEW TOWN: Less atmospheric neighborhood, but choose from Art Nouveau decor to the latest international cuisine.	
⑱	**$$$ Restaurace u Pinkasů** Jungmannovo Náměstí 16 tel. 221-111-150	Pilsner beer since 1843, traditional interior or shaded garden, lunch specials, rude waiters
⑲	**$$ Hospoda u Nováka** V Jirchářích 2 tel. 224-930-639	Pub with few tourists, many regulars, classic Czech fare, cheap unlisted specials
⑳	**$ Kavárna Muzeum** Vinohradská 1 tel. 224-284-511	Daily specials and sandwiches in pleasant kid-friendly setting

㉑	**$$$ Municipal House** Náměstí Republiky 5 tel. 222-002-763 (café) tel. 222-002-777 (restaurant)	Art Nouveau concert hall has dressy café (best for salad or drinks), pricey French restaurant, touristy beer cellar

LITTLE QUARTER: Characteristic eateries in atmospheric cobble-stoned lanes, nice for your pre- or post-castle visit. If browsing on your own, try Kampa Square, just south of the Charles Bridge.

㉒	**$$ Malostranská Beseda** Malostranské Náměstí 21 tel. 257-409-112	Wide-ranging menu, eat in restaurant or café or packed beerhall, music club upstairs
㉓	**$$ Lokál u Bílé Kuželky** Míšeňská 12 tel. 257-212-014	Quick, cheap well-executed Czech classics, non-smoking section
㉔	**$$ Lo Veg Restaurant** Nerudova 36 mobile 702-901-060	Vegan take on Czech classics in tasteful setting with view
㉕	**$ U Hrocha** Thunovská 10 tel. 257-533-389	Small authentic pub for beer, small-plate meats, daily specials, politician hangout
㉖	**$$$ Čertovka** U Lužického Semináře 24 tel. 257-534-524	Outdoor terrace views of the Charles Bridge, reasonable specials, arrive early (no reservations)
㉗	**$ Cukrkávalimonáda** Lázeňská 7 tel. 257-225-396	Oasis from the touristy Charles Bridge, salads and ciabatta sandwiches in old/new decor

CASTLE QUARTER: My listings either boast views or are handy for your castle visit.

㉘	**$$$ Bellavista Restaurant** At Strahov Monastery tel. 220-517-274	Amazing city views (in good weather), garden setting, reasonably priced grilled meats, pasta, and salads
㉙	**$$-$$$ Villa Richter** Down the stairs from castle tour exit tel. 257-219-079	These three restaurants all have stunning views, prices and menus range from sandwiches to midrange Czech fare to pricey French

Eating

30	**$$ U Labutí** Hradčanské Náměstí 11 tel. 220-511-191	Czech food, good price, tranquil courtyard, on Castle Square
31	**$ Café Salmovský Palác** Hradčanské Náměstí 1 mobile 725-816-267	Soups and pasta and coffee with great views, on Castle Square
32	**$ Kavárna ve Šternberském Paláci** Hradčanské Náměstí 15 mobile 721-138-290	Locals' getaway on Castle Square (tucked behind Archbishop's Palace), soup and goulash

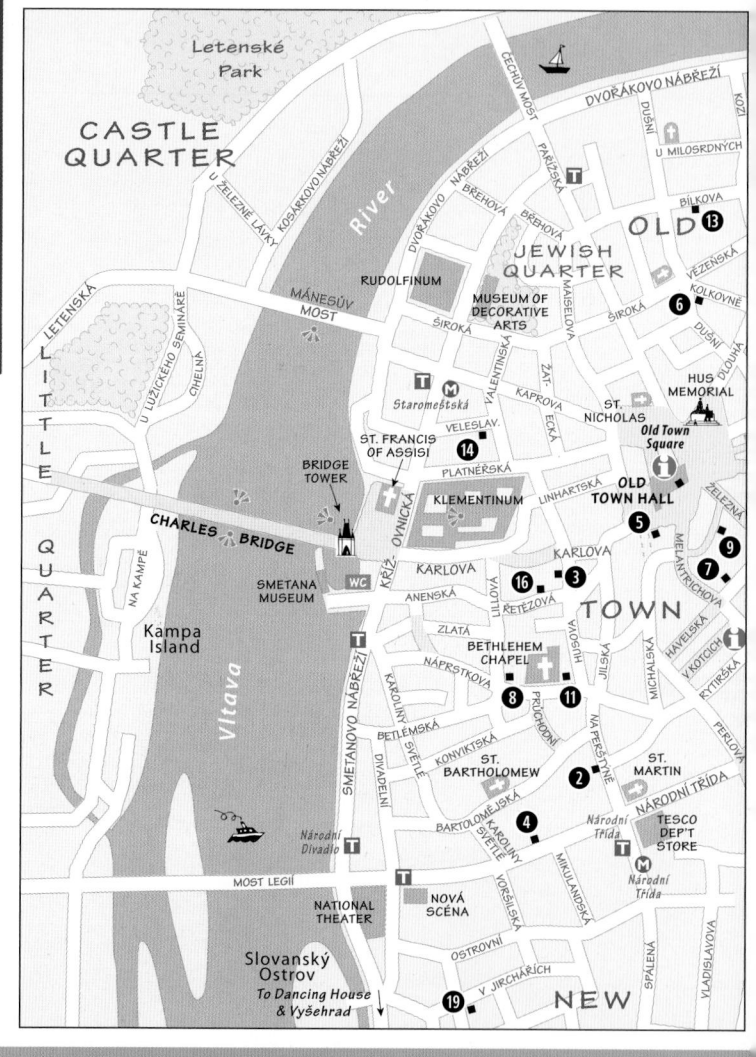

Restaurants in Old & New Towns

Eating

ST. AGNES CONVENT

RÁSNOVKA

ZA HAŠTALEM

HRADEBNÍ

REVOLUČNÍ

SOUKENICKÁ

WILSONOVA

17

10

HAŠTALSKÁ

KOZÍ

DLOUHÁ

RYBNÁ

MASNÁ

BENEDIKT.

PALLADIUM MALL

200 Meters

200 Yards

ŠTUPARTSKÁ

ST. JAMES

RYBNÁ

JAKUBSKÁ

TEMPLOVÁ

KRÁLODVORSKÁ

Republic Square

NA FLORENCI

12

ŠTUP.

WC

Ungelt

MUNICIPAL HOUSE

NEW

MASARYK STATION

TÝN CHURCH

CELETNÁ

CELETNÁ

21

Náměstí Republiky

HYBERNSKÁ

KAROLINUM

POWDER TOWER

TOWN

15

Ovocný Trh

D.LÁŽENÁ

OPLETALOVA

BOLZANOVA

NA PŘÍKOPĚ

SENOVÁŽNÁ

HAVELSKÁ ULIČKA

HAVÍŘSKÁ

NEKÁZANKA

JINDŘIŠSKÁ

JERUZALÉMSKÁ

JERUSALEM SYNAGOGUE

1

NA MŮSTKU

ČERNÁ RŮŽE MALL

PANSKÁ

Jindřišská

MUSEUM OF COMMUNISM

MUCHA MUSEUM

U PŮJČOVNY

RŮŽOVÁ

Hlavní Nádraží

MAIN TRAIN STATION

28. ŘÍJNA

Můstek

JINDŘIŠSKÁ

18

POST

PANSKÁ

ST. MARY OF THE SNOWS

Wenceslas Square

Můstek

GRAND HOTEL EVROPA

Franciscan Garden

OPLETALOVA

WASHINGTONOVA

JINDŘIŠSKÁ

PALACKÉHO

LUCERNA ARCADE

VODIČKOVA

ŠTĚPÁNSKÁ

JUNGMANNOVA

WILSONOVA

VINOHRADY

TOWN

20

Rick Steves | Pocket Prague

Restaurants in the Little Quarter & Castle Quarter

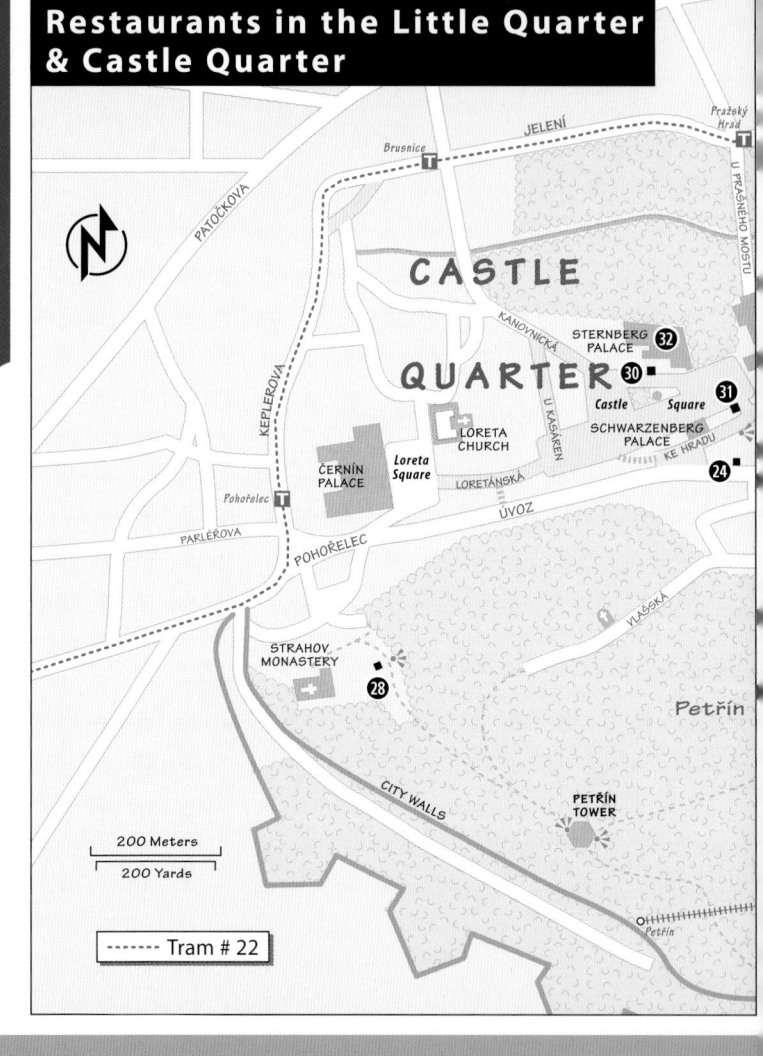

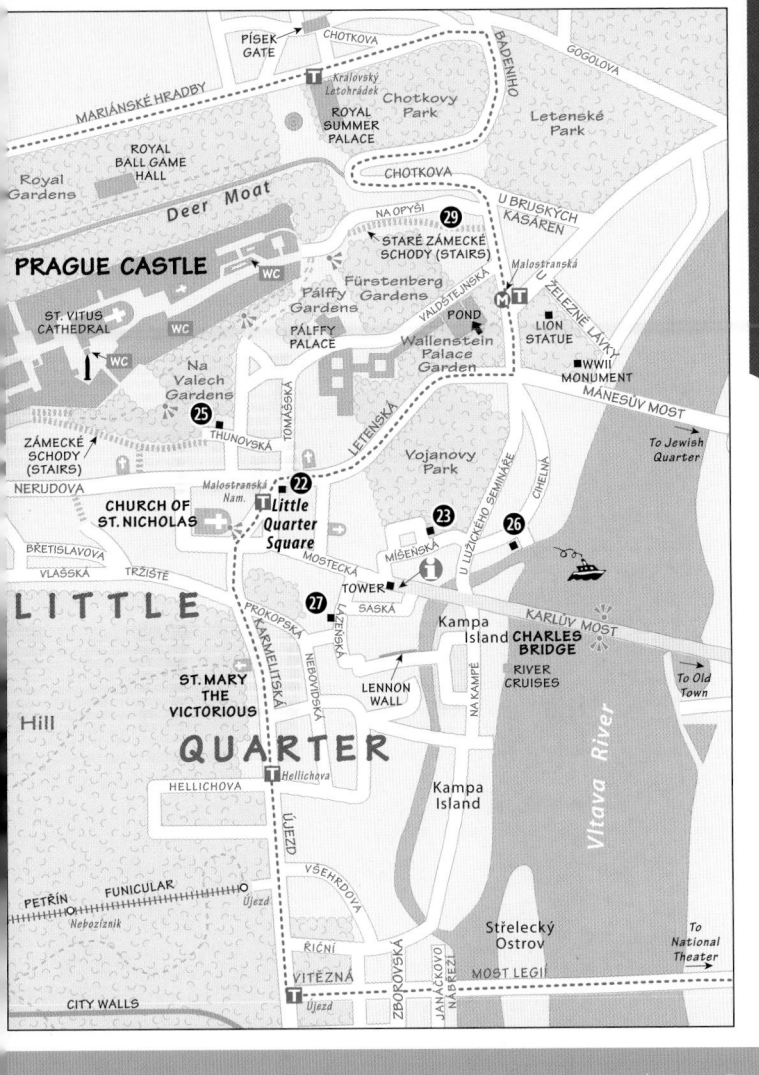

PÍSEK GATE

CHOTKOVA

BADENÍHO

GOGOLOVA

MARIÁNSKÉ HRADBY

Královský Letohrádek

ROYAL SUMMER PALACE

Chotkovy Park

Letenské Park

ROYAL BALL GAME HALL

CHOTKOVA

Royal Gardens

Deer Moat

NA OPYŠI

U BRUSKÝCH KASÁREN

PRAGUE CASTLE

STARÉ ZÁMECKÉ SCHODY (STAIRS)

29

Malostranská

M

WC

Fürstenberg Gardens

Pálffy Gardens

VALDŠTEJNSKÁ

POND

U ŽELEZNÉ LÁVKY

ST. VITUS CATHEDRAL

WC

PÁLFFY PALACE

Wallenstein Palace Garden

LION STATUE

WC

Na Valech Gardens

LETENSKÁ

WWII MONUMENT

MÁNESŮV MOST

TOMÁŠSKÁ

25

ZÁMECKÉ SCHODY (STAIRS)

THUNOVSKÁ

Vojanovy Park

To Jewish Quarter

NERUDOVA

Malostranská Nám.

22 Little Quarter Square

23

U LUŽICKÉHO SEMINÁŘE

CIHELNÁ

26

CHURCH OF ST. NICHOLAS

BŘETISLAVOVA

MÍŠENSKÁ

i

VLAŠSKÁ

TRŽIŠTĚ

MOSTECKÁ

TOWER

SASKÁ

KARLŮV MOST

LITTLE

PROKOPSKÁ

LÁZEŇSKÁ

Kampa Island

CHARLES BRIDGE

To Old Town

27

Lennon Wall

NA KAMPĚ

RIVER CRUISES

ST. MARY THE VICTORIOUS

KARMELITSKÁ

NEBOVIDSKÁ

QUARTER

Hill

HELLICHOVA

Hellichova

Kampa Island

Vltava River

ÚJEZD

VŠEHRDOVA

PETŘÍN FUNICULAR

Nebozízek

ŘÍČNÍ

Střelecký Ostrov

To National Theater

CITY WALLS

VÍTĚZNÁ

Újezd

ZBOROVSKÁ

JANÁČKOVO NÁBŘEŽÍ

MOST LEGII

Practicalities

PLANNING

Prague's best travel months—also the busiest and most expensive for flights and hotels—are from April through October. May, June, and September have the most festivals and biggest crowds (making hotel bookings tougher). July and August offer the best weather, longer days, and fewer tourists. September and early October have mild weather. Winter travelers find the concert season in full swing, with significantly fewer tourists. December brings Christmas markets, fragrant with the scent of hot wine with cloves. Prague explodes with fun on New Year's Eve, teeming with thousands of foreign visitors (booking up hotels). January and February have few tourists, an occasional dusting of snow, and plum brandy and hot wine in the pubs. By April, Prague turns green again and the tourists start arriving.

Make sure your passport is up to date (to renew, see travel.state. gov). Call your debit- and credit-card companies about your plans. Book hotel rooms well in advance, especially for peak season—May, June, and September. Consider buying travel insurance. If you're traveling beyond Prague, research rail passes, train reservations, and car rentals.

Helpful Websites

Tourist Information: For Prague only: Prague.eu; for the country, Czechtourism.com

Passports and Red Tape: Travel.state.gov

Cheap Flights: Kayak.com (for international flights), Skyscanner.com (for flights within Europe)

Airplane Carry-on Restrictions: Tsa.gov

European Train Schedules: Bahn.com

General Travel Tips: Ricksteves.com (helpful info on train travel, rail passes, car rental, using your mobile device, travel insurance, packing lists, and much more—plus updates to this book)

MONEY

The Czech Republic uses the currency called the crown or *koruna* (pronounced koh-ROH-nah, and abbreviated Kč). 1 Kč = about a nickel, so 20 Kč = $1. To roughly convert crowns to dollars, drop the last digit and divide in half. (Check Oanda.com for the latest exchange rates.)

Withdraw money from an ATM (known as a *Bankomat* in the Czech Republic) using a debit card, just like at home. Visa and MasterCard are commonly used throughout Europe. Before departing, call your bank or credit-card company: Ask about international transaction fees, and alert them that you'll be making withdrawals in Europe. Many travelers bring a second debit/credit card as a backup. Cash is always good to have on hand, so try to withdraw large amounts (7,000-8,000 Kč) from the ATM. American magnetic-stripe credit cards are accepted everywhere in the Czech Republic (as the Czech Republic has not yet adopted the newer chip-and-PIN cards common in much of Europe). Regardless, it's always wise to be prepared for some transactions with cash.

To keep your cash and valuables safe, wear a money belt. But if you do lose your credit or debit card, report your loss immediately. Call these 24-hour US numbers collect: Visa (tel. 303/967-1096), MasterCard (tel. 636/722-7111), and American Express (tel. 336/393-1111). In the Czech Republic, to make a collect call to the US, dial 00-800-222-55288; press zero or stay on the line for an English-speaking operator.

ATMs work just like at home.

The *koruna* is worth about a nickel.

ARRIVAL IN PRAGUE

By Train at the Main Train Station (Hlavní Nádraží)

Prague's **Main Station** is Hlavní Nádraží (or "Praha hl. n." on schedules). All international trains arrive here, as do most trains within the Czech Republic (including high-speed SC Pendolino trains), as well as buses to and from Nürnberg and Munich.

The station is a hive of shops and services. From the train, go through any of the three tunnels to the main arrival hall. Here you'll find the Metro entrances. An ATM (with better rates than any of the exchange offices) is along the right wall; two more are under the central stairs. Lockers are in the corner under the stairs on the right, and a Billa supermarket is in the corner under the stairs to the left. The Touristpoint office—at the left end of the main hall (as you face the tracks)—offers a last-minute room-finding service, books car rentals, and sells maps, international phone cards, sightseeing tours, and adrenaline experiences. Perhaps most importantly, they're willing to call you a taxi (Touristpoint open daily 8:00-22:00, tel. 224-946-010, www.touristpoint.cz). If you need to buy train tickets, you'll find the Czech Railways (České Dráhy) ticket office—marked *ČD Centrum*—in the middle of the main hall under the stairs.

The busy Main Train Station has Old World class and modern tourist services.

Getting from the Main Train Station to Your Hotel

Even though the Main Train Station is basically downtown, getting to your hotel can be a little tricky. On foot is simplest (if tiring). The Metro and trams work great if they stop near your destination. Taxi is the easiest and priciest; be sure to follow my tips.

On Foot: Most hotels I list in the Old Town are within a 20-minute walk of the train station. Exit the station into a small park, walk through the park, and then cross the street on the other side. Head down Jeruzalémská street to the Jindřišská Tower and tram stop, walk under a small arch, then continue slightly to the right down Senovážná street. At the end of the street, you'll see the Powder Tower—the grand entry into the Old Town—to the left. Alternatively, Wenceslas Square in the New Town is a 10-minute walk—exit the station, cross the park, and walk to the left along Opletalova street.

By Metro: The Metro is easy. In the main hall are the entrances to the Metro (marked with a red *M*) going two directions: *Háje* or *Letňany*. Buy tickets from the machine by the Metro entrance (you'll need Czech coins; get change at the change machine in the corner near the luggage lockers, or break a bill at a newsstand or grocery). Validate your ticket in the yellow machines *before* you go down the stairs to the tracks. To get to hotels in the Old Town, catch a Háje-bound train to the Muzeum stop, then transfer to the green line (direction: Dejvická) and get off at either Můstek or Staroměstská; these stops straddle the Old Town. The next stop, Malostranská, is handy for hotels in the Little Quarter. For more information on the Metro, see page 170.

Taxi: The fair metered rate into the Old Town is about 200 Kč; if your hotel is farther out or across the river, it should be no more than 300 Kč. Avoid the "official" taxi stand that's marked inside the station: These thugs routinely overcharge arriving tourists. Instead, to get an **honest cabbie,** exit the station's main hall through the big glass doors, then cross 50 yards through a park to Opletalova street. A few taxis are usually waiting there in front of Hotel Chopin, on the corner of Jeruzalémská street. Alternatively, the Touristpoint office, described earlier, can call a taxi for you. Or call a taxi yourself: AAA Taxi—tel. 222-333-222; City Taxi—tel. 257-257-257. Before getting into a taxi, always confirm the maximum price to your destination, and make sure the driver turns on the meter. For more pointers on taking taxis, see page 170.

By Tram: The nearest tram stop is to the right as you exit the station (about 200 yards away). Tram #9 (headed away from railway tracks) takes you to the neighborhood near the National Theater and the Little Quarter, but isn't useful for most Old Town hotels.

By Plane at Václav Havel Airport

Prague's modern, tidy, user-friendly Václav Havel Airport (formerly Ruzyně Airport) is located 12 miles (about 30 minutes) west of the city center. Terminal 2 serves destinations within the EU except for Great Britain (no passport controls). Terminal 1 serves Great Britain and everywhere else. The airport has the normal services: ATMs (avoid the change desks), shops and cafés, kiosks selling city maps and phone cards, and a TI with few printed materials (airport code: PRG, airport tel. 220-113-314, operator tel. 220-111-111, www.prg.aero/en).

Getting from the Airport to Your Hotel

From either airport terminal, you have four options:

Čedaz Shuttle Bus: This airport minibus goes to the Náměstí Republiky Metro stop, a 5-minute walk to the Old Town. The shuttle stops on V Celnici street, across the street from Hotel Marriott. From the airport, catch the bus from exit F at Terminal 1 or exit E at Terminal 2 and pay the driver directly (130 Kč, daily 7:30-19:00, 2/hour, 30-minute ride, info desk in arrival hall).

AE Shuttle Bus: This airport shuttle bus stops at the Main Train Station (see earlier) and the Masarykovo Nádraží train station (a 7-minute walk to the Old Town). From either stop, you can catch the Metro or a taxi, or walk to your destination. Look for the *AE* sign in front of the airport terminal and pay the driver (50 Kč, daily 5:46-21:16, 2/hour, 40-minute ride, www.cd.cz/en).

Taxi: The metered rate is generally 500-600 Kč to downtown—confirm the cost before you get in. Cabbies wait at the curb directly in front of the arrival hall. Or book a yellow AAA taxi through their office in the airport hall—you'll get a 50 percent discount coupon for the trip back (book your return trip by calling 222-333-222). AAA taxis wait in front of exit D at Terminal 1 and exit E at Terminal 2. For a friendly, reasonably priced private taxi, try **Mike's Chauffeur Service,** listed on page 170.

Bus and Metro (Cheap but Slow): Take bus #119 to the Nádraží Veleslavín stop or #100 to the Zličín Metro station (20 minutes), then take the Metro into the center (32 Kč, buy tickets at info desk in airport arrival hall).

HELPFUL HINTS

Tourist Information (TI): The main TI is on the **Old Town Square** in the Old Town Hall, just to the left of the Astronomical Clock (open Easter-Oct Mon-Fri 9:00-19:00, Sat-Sun 9:00-18:00; Nov-Easter Mon-Fri 9:00-18:00, Sat-Sun 9:00-17:00). Other TI branches are on the castle side of the **Charles Bridge** (Easter-Oct only) and by the **Havelská Market** (April-Oct only). For general tourist information in English, dial 221-714-444 (Mon-Fri 8:00-19:00), or check the useful TI website: www.praguewelcome.cz.

The TIs offer maps, a helpful transit guide, and information on guided walks and bus tours. They can book local guides, concerts, and occasionally hotel rooms. Pick up at least one of the monthly event guides (e.g., *Prague Guide, Prague This Month*). The English-language weekly *Prague Post* newspaper also has entertainment listings and current events (60 Kč at newsstands, or read online at www.praguepost.com).

Hurdling the Language Barrier: Believe me, if you learn even a handful of Czech phrases, your interactions with locals will be much nicer. Learn "Hello" (*Dobrý den;* DOH-bree dehn), "Please" (*Prosím;* PROH-seem), "Thank you" (*Děkuji;* DYACK-kwee) and "Goodbye" (*Nashledanou;* NAH-skleh-dah-noh). To learn a few more Czech phrases, see page 183.

The area by the Old Town Hall is a hub of tourist services and sightseeing options.

Tipping

Tipping in the Czech Republic isn't as generous as it is in the US. To tip a taxi driver, round up about 5 percent, if you wish. At hotels, if you let the porter carry your luggage or someone does something especially nice for you, you could tip about 50 Kč (or not at
all). For sit-down service in a restaurant, a service charge is generally already included in the list price of the food. However, if you feel the service was exceptional, it's fine to tip 5-10 percent extra.

Practicalities

Time: The Czech Republic's time zone is six/nine hours ahead of the east/west coasts of the US.

Business Hours: Most stores are open Monday through Friday from roughly 9:00 or 10:00 until 17:00 or 18:00, Saturday morning until lunch-time, and closed Sunday. Souvenir shops in Prague's Old Town, and other businesses serving both urbanites and tourists (like small grocery stores), are open daily until at least 20:00.

Watt's Up? Europe's electrical system is 220 volts, instead of North America's 110 volts. You'll need to bring an adapter plug with two round prongs, sold inexpensively at travel stores in the US. Most newer electronics (such as mobile devices, laptops, hair dryers, and battery chargers) convert automatically, so you won't need a separate converter.

Numbers and Stumblers: What Americans call the second floor of a building is the first floor in Europe. Europeans write dates as day/month/year. Commas are decimal points and vice versa—a dollar and half is 1,50, and there are 5.280 feet in a mile. The Czech Republic uses the metric system: A kilogram is 2.2 pounds; a liter is about a quart; and a kilometer is six-tenths of a mile. Temperature is measured in Celsius: 0°C = 32°F. To roughly convert Celsius to Fahrenheit, double the number and add 30.

Addresses: Prague is administratively carved up into numerical districts. Almost everything of interest to tourists is in "Praha 1," in the old center on both sides of the river. If an address says "Dukelských Hrdinů 48, Praha 7," it's in the seventh district.

Best Views: Enjoy the "Golden City of a Hundred Spires" during the early evening, when the light is warm and the colors are rich. Good viewpoints include: Prague Castle, the Strahov Monastery, the Villa Richter restaurants (near the castle), the Charles Bridge towers, the Old Town Square clock tower, and Hotel u Prince's rooftop restaurant.

Bookstores: Shakespeare and Sons is a friendly English-language bookstore (including English translations from Czech) with a reading space overlooking a river channel (daily 11:00-19:00, one block from the Charles Bridge on Little Quarter side at U Lužického Semináře 10, tel. 257-531-894, www.shakes.cz). The small **Franz Kafka Society** bookshop (in the heart of the Jewish Quarter) also has Czech lit in English translations (daily 10:00-18:00, Široká 14, tel. 224-227-452).

Maps: A good map of Prague is essential. Get one with trams, buses, and Metro lines marked, and tiny sketches of the sights drawn in—I like the *Kartografie Praha* city map, but other brands will do (30-70 Kč, sold at kiosks and tobacco stands). A **mapping app** for your smartphone (e.g., City Maps 2Go) can pinpoint your location using GPS. To avoid data-roaming charges, look for an offline map that can be downloaded in its entirety before your trip.

Laundry: A full-service laundry near many recommended hotels is 200 yards south of the Charles Bridge on the Old Town side at Karolíny Světlé 11 (200 Kč/8-pound load, wash and dry in 3 hours, Mon-Fri 7:30-19:00, closed Sat-Sun, mobile 721-030-446). Or ask your hotelier for the closest laundry.

Buying Essentials: For your grocery needs, you'll find plenty of

Invest in a good map with transit lines.

Explore by following pictographic signs.

corner convenience stores everywhere, generally open daily until midnight. For anything else, try the big Tesco department store, located between the Old and New Towns (daily 8:00-20:00, Národní Třída 26).

Local Help: Magic Praha is an all-purpose travel service that can help with accommodations and transportation throughout the Czech Republic, as well as private tours and side-trips to historic towns (mobile 604-207-225, www.magicpraha.cz, magicpraha@magicpraha.cz).

GETTING AROUND PRAGUE

You can walk nearly everywhere. Brown street signs (in Czech, but with helpful little icons) direct you to tourist landmarks. To walk from the Old Town Square to the Charles Bridge takes less than 10 minutes.

Still, it's worth figuring out the excellent public transportation system, especially the trams. Be bold, and you'll swing through Prague like Tarzan. Make sure your city map has public-transit routes marked.

By Metro, Tram, and Bus

Tickets: The Metro, trams, and buses all use the same tickets:

- 30-minute **short-trip ticket** *(krátkodobá),* which allows as many transfers as you can make in a half hour—24 Kč

- 90-minute **standard ticket** *(základní)*—32 Kč

- **24-hour pass** *(jízdenka na 24 hodin)*—110 Kč

- **3-day pass** *(jízdenka na 3 dny)*—310 Kč

Buy tickets from your hotel, at Metro stops, newsstand kiosks, or from machines (select ticket price, then insert coins). To avoid wasting time

Learn a few handy tram lines.

Tram #22 works as a self-guided city tour.

looking for a ticket-seller when your tram is approaching, stock up on all the tickets that you think you'll need. Since Prague is a walkable town, most visitors find that individual tickets work better than a pass.

Be sure to validate your ticket as you board the tram or bus, or as you enter the Metro station, by sticking it in the machine, which stamps a time on it—watch locals and imitate. Inspectors routinely ambush ticket-less riders (including tourists) and fine them 700 Kč on the spot.

The Metro closes at midnight, but some night trams run all night. You can find more info in English at www.dpp.cz.

By Tram

Navigate by signs that list the end stations. At the platform, a sign lists all the stops for each tram in order. Remember that trams going one direction leave from one platform, while the other direction might leave from a different platform nearby—maybe across the street or a half-block away. When the tram arrives, open the doors by pressing the green button. Once aboard, validate your ticket in the machine.

As you go, follow along carefully so you know when your stop comes up. Newer trams have electronic signs that show either the next stop (*příští*), or a list of upcoming stops. Also, listen to the recorded announcements for the name of the stop you're currently at, followed by the name of the stop that's coming up next. (Confused tourists, thinking they've heard their stop, are notorious for rushing off the tram one stop too soon.) The surest way to know whether it's your stop is to check the platform for a sign that shows the name of the stop. Even better, use a mapping app on your smartphone so you'll always know where you are.

Handy Trams: These lines are especially useful.

• **Tram #22** is practically made for sightseeing, connecting the New Town with the Castle Quarter and stopping near many major landmarks. (See my "Self-Guided Tram Tour," on page 126.)

• **Tram #17** runs roughly north-south through the Old Town and north to Mucha's *Slav Epic*.

• **Tram #18** connects the Little Quarter and Castle Quarter (at the Malostranská stop) with the Old Town, then cuts south through the New Town.

• **Tram #24** is helpful for reaching the *Slav Epic* from Wenceslas Square.

By Metro

The three-line Metro system is handy and simple, but doesn't always get you right to the tourist sights (landmarks such as the Old Town Square and Prague Castle are several blocks from the nearest Metro stops). Although it seems that all Metro doors lead to the neighborhood of Výstup, that's simply the Czech word for "exit."

By Taxi

I find Prague to be a great taxi town and use them routinely. That said, the city has more than its share of dishonest cabbies, so here are a few tips to avoid being overcharged.

The legitimate rates are cheap: Drop charge 40 Kč, then 30 Kč per-kilometer charge, and waiting time 6 Kč/minute. These rates are clearly marked on the door, so be sure the cabbie honors them. Also insist that cabbies turn on the meter, and that it's set at the right tariff, or *"sazba"* (usually but not always tariff #1). Unlike in many cities, there's no extra charge for calling a cab—the meter starts only after you get in. Tip by rounding up; locals never tip more than 5 percent.

Have a ballpark idea of what your ride will cost and confirm an approximate fare with the cabbie before getting inside. Figure about 150-200 Kč for a ride between landmarks within the city center (for example, from the Main Train Station to the Old Town Square, or from the Charles Bridge to the castle). Even the longest ride in the center should cost under 300 Kč.

To improve your odds of getting a fair metered rate, call for a cab (or ask someone at your hotel or restaurant to call one for you), rather than hailing one on the street. **AAA Taxi** (tel. 222-333-222) and **City Taxi** (tel. 257-257-257) are the most likely to have English-speaking staff and honest cabbies. Hailing a passing taxi usually gets me a more honest price than taking one waiting like a vulture at a tourist attraction or train station.

And what if the cabbie surprises you at the end with an astronomical fare? Challenge it. Point to the rates on the door. Get your hotel receptionist to back you up. Get out your phone and threaten to call the police (tel. 158); because of new legislation to curb dishonest cabbies, the police will stand up for you. Or simply pay what you think the ride should cost—as mentioned, 300 Kč should cover you for a long ride anywhere in the center—and walk away.

Mike's Chauffeur Service offers a reliable, family-run taxi service with fair and fixed rates around town, on day trips outside Prague, and travel to destinations around the Czech Republic and beyond (tel. 241-768-231, mobile 602-224-893, www.mike-chauffeur.cz, mike.chauffeur@cmail.cz).

On Bike
Prague has a decent network of bike paths, making bicycles a feasible option for exploring the center of the town and beyond (see http://wgp.praha-mesto.cz for a map). Two companies near the Old Town Square rent bikes for about 300 Kč for two hours or 500 Kč per day (with a 1,500-Kč deposit), and also organize guided bike tours. They are Praha Bike (daily 9:00-22:00, Dlouhá 24, mobile 732-388-880, www.prahabike.cz) and City Bike (daily 9:00-19:00, Králodvorská 5, mobile 776-180-284, www.citybike-prague.com).

Car Rental
You won't want to drive within compact Prague, but a car can be handy for exploring the countryside. It's generally best to arrange car rental before your trip from a major company (Hertz, Avis, etc.), but you can also do it in Prague; all the big companies have offices here. A locally operated alternative—with great bargains on their cheaper models—is Prima Rent (Mon-Fri 8:00-16:30, closed Sat-Sun, Kolbenova 40, Metro: Kolbenova, mobile 602-608-494, www.primarent.cz).

COMMUNICATING

Telephones and Internet
Making Calls: To call the Czech Republic from the US or Canada: Dial 011 (our international access code), then 420 (the Czech Republic's country code), and then the local number, without the initial zero. To call the Czech Republic from a European country: Dial 00 (Europe's international access code), then 420 followed by the local number, without the initial zero. To call within the Czech Republic, just dial the nine-digit number. To call from the Czech Republic to another country: Dial 00, the country code (for example, 1 for the US or Canada), then the area code and number. If you're calling European countries whose phone numbers begin with 0, you'll usually have to omit that 0 when you dial. If you're calling anywhere

Practicalities

Useful Contacts

Police: Tel. 158

Emergency Medical Assistance: Tel. 112

US Embassy: Tel. 257-022-000 (24-hour line), emergency passport services Mon-Fri 8:00-11:30, in Prague's Little Quarter below the castle at Tržiště 15, http://prague.usembassy.gov, ACSPrg@state.gov

Canadian Embassy: Tel. 272-101-800, consular services Mon-Thu 9:00-12:00, Fri and afternoons by appointment, north of the Castle Quarter at Ve Struhách 95/2, www.canadainternational.gc.ca/czech-tcheque, prgue-cs@international.gc.ca

Directory Assistance: Tel. 1188 (12-27 Kč/minute)

Internet "Yellow Pages" and "White Pages": www.zlatestranky.cz

from Europe using your US mobile phone, you may need to dial as if you're calling from the US.

Phoning Inexpensively: Since coin-op pay phones are nearly obsolete, you'll need an international phone card (150 Kč and up). With this, you can make reasonably priced local and international calls from any pay phone, from a European mobile phone, and even from your hotel phone (though some hotels block these cards or charge a fee). Buy cards at newsstands, electronics stores, and Internet cafés. Tell the vendor where you'll be making the most calls (to America), and he'll select a good-value brand (Smartcall is widely available). When using an international phone card, you always must dial the area code, even if you're calling across the street. Calling from your hotel room without a phone card can be a rip-off—ask your hotelier about their rates before you dial.

Mobile Phones, Smartphones, Internet: Many US mobile phones work in Europe. Expect to pay around $1.50 a minute for phone calls and 30 cents per text message (somewhat less if you sign up for an international calling plan with your service provider). It's easy to buy a phone in Europe, which costs more up front but is cheaper by the call. You'll find mobile-phone stores selling cheap phones (for as little as $20 plus minutes) and SIM cards at Prague's airport, major train stations, and throughout Prague.

Smartphones give you access to the Internet and travel-oriented apps—helpful for planning your sightseeing, emailing hotels, and staying in touch. You can make free or cheap phone calls using Skype (sign up at skype.com), Google Talk (google.com/talk), or FaceTime (preloaded on many Apple devices). City Maps 2Go gives you good searchable maps even when you're not online ($2, available from iTunes).

To avoid sky-high fees for data roaming, disable data roaming entirely, and only go online when you have free Wi-Fi (e.g., at your hotel or in a café). Or you could sign up for an international data plan for the duration of your trip: $30 typically buys about 100 megabytes—enough to view 100 websites or send/receive 1,000 emails.

Most hotels offer some form of free or cheap Internet access—either a shared computer in the lobby or Wi-Fi in the room. Otherwise, your hotelier can point you to the nearest Internet café. (To switch a Czech-alphabet keyboard to English, click on the "CZ" at the bottom of the screen to toggle to "EN.") You'll also find Wi-Fi hotspots at cafés (when you order something, ask the waiter for the Wi-Fi password).

For more information, talk to your service provider or see ricksteves.com/phoning.

SIGHTSEEING TIPS

Hours: Hours of sights can change unexpectedly; confirm the latest times with the TI, the sight's website, or the city's website (Prague.eu). Many sights stop admitting people 30-60 minutes before closing time, and guards start shooing people out before the actual closing time, so don't save the best for last.

What to Expect: Some sights may have metal detectors or conduct bag searches that will slow your entry. Others require you to check (for free) daypacks and coats. If you hope to avoid checking a small backpack, carry it under your arm like a purse as you enter.

Photos and videos are normally allowed, but flashes or tripods usually are not. Some Czech sights charge a photography fee. Many sights offer guided tours and rent audioguides. Expect changes—artwork can be in restoration or on tour. Most sights have an on-site café.

Discounts: Many sights offer free or reduced admission for children under 18 and for students (with International Student Identity Cards, isic.org). Senior discounts are generally only for EU residents, but it's worth asking.

Free Rick Steves Audio Tours: I've produced free audio tours of many of Europe's best sights. With a mobile device, you can take me along for the Prague City Walk—from Wenceslas Square to Charles Bridge. Download the tour via the Rick Steves Audio Europe smartphone app, ricksteves.com/audioeurope, iTunes, or Google Play.

Prague Card: This pricey sightseeing pass (e.g., €48 for 2 days) is usually not worth the cost for most travelers, but it might fit your itinerary. Here are some of the things it covers: public transit (including the airport bus); admission or discounts to a number of sights (including Prague Castle and Jewish Quarter sights); a free bus tour and river cruise; and discounts to other attractions, concerts and guided tours. If that list looks promising, get all the details (pick up a brochure at the TI, or go to www.praguecard.com and try their calculator feature), and do the math.

THEFT AND EMERGENCIES

Theft: While violent crime is rare in the city center, thieves (mainly pickpockets) thrive near famous monuments, on public transportation, at places of drunkenness, in hostels, or anywhere crowds press together. Be alert to the possibility of theft, even when you're absorbed in the wonder and newness of Prague. Smartphones are thief-magnets. Pickpockets can be little children or adults dressed as business professionals or even as tourists. Any commotion in a crowd may actually be a smokescreen for theft. Plainclothes policemen "looking for counterfeit money" are con artists. I keep my valuables—passport, credit cards, crucial documents, and large amounts of cash—in a money belt that I tuck under my beltline.

Most scams fall into the category of being charged a two-scoop price for one scoop of ice cream, having extra items appear on your restaurant bill, or not getting the correct change. Get comfortable with that *koruna*-to-dollar exchange rate and know approximately how much you should be charged. Beware the "slow count," where clerks give back part of your change, then pause...hoping you'll think they're done and you'll leave before getting all your change. All of this can sound intimidating, but Prague is safe. Simply stay alert.

Dial 158 for English-speaking police help. To replace a passport, file the police report, then contact your embassy (see "Useful Contacts" on page 172).

Medical Help: Dial 112 for a medical emergency. Most doctors speak English. Your hotelier can assist you in finding care. For minor ailments, do as the Czechs do and first visit a pharmacy, where qualified technicians routinely diagnose and prescribe. There's a 24-hour pharmacy near Wenceslas Square at Palackého 5 (tel. 224-946-982). For above-standard assistance in English (including dental service), consider Hospital Na Homolce (less than 1,000 Kč for appointment, call 252-922-146 if between the hours of 8:00-16:00, for after-hours emergencies call 257-211-111).

ACTIVITIES

Shopping

Prague's entire Old Town seems designed to bring out the shopper in visitors. Strolling the lanes and browsing the specialty stores is a kind of sightseeing, even if you never buy. Most shops are open Monday through Saturday 9:00 to 17:00 (or later), closed Sunday, and some also close Saturday afternoon.

Shopping Neighborhoods: Ground zero is the **Old Town Square** area. Browse the Ungelt courtyard (tucked behind the Týn Church), packed with touristy but decent-quality shops. Celetná street offers all the traditional Czech goodies. On the other hand, Karlova street is clogged with tourists and cheap-o trinkets, and should be avoided entirely. (Psst! Near the Astronomical Clock, sneak through the big stone gateway marked *459*. This leads to Michalská, a semi-hidden lane of shops a bit off the tourist crush.)

Two blocks south of the Old Town Square is the open-air **Havelská Market,** a touristy but enjoyable place for inexpensive handicrafts and fresh produce (daily 9:00-18:00).

The street separating the Old and New Towns—**Na Příkopě**—has modern shopping malls. The best is Slovanský Dům (at #22), with a peaceful inner courtyard. Nearby, on Náměstí Republiky (Republic Square) is Prague's biggest mall, called Palladium, and the communist-era department store Kotva, an obsolete beast. Walking westward (where the street is called Národní Třída), you'll find less touristy stores.

For high-fashion clothing and design stores (both Czech and international), explore the **Jewish Quarter,** particularly Pařížská street and the side-streets that run parallel to Pařížská (Eliški Krásnohorské street and Dušní street). Closer to the Old Town Square is Dlouhá street.

Souvenirs

The most traditional Czech handicrafts are puppets, glass and crystal, and garnets. More recently, they've become known for unique fashion and design, particularly in the Art Nouveau style.

Czech Puppets: Made of local linden wood, these have been treasured here for centuries. During times of foreign occupation, traveling puppeteers kept the Czech language, humor, and culture alive. Czech grandfathers passed their puppet-making designs on to their grandsons. In communist times, puppets poked fun at puppet governments. Today, the arts of puppet-making and puppet theater are still alive. You can buy an inexpensive jester, witch, or Pinocchio anywhere in town. For higher quality ($100 and up), try the Marionety Truhlář shop at the west end of Charles Bridge (U Lužického Semináře 5, www.marionety.com) or the nearby Galerie Michael (U Lužického Semináře 7, www.marionettes michael.cz). In the Ungelt courtyard, browse the shop called Hračky, Loutky.

Glass and Crystal: The exquisite glassware called lead crystal is glass fortified with at least 24 percent lead oxide. The lead gives the glass that special sparkle, adds weight, makes it easier to cut, and produces a harmonious "ding-gg" when you flick it. A cheaper product called "crystal glass" is similar but has a smaller percentage of lead. You'll see all kinds of decoration and colors, or cut with facets like a diamond. The most traditional Czech pattern looks like intricate lace or tight rows of starbursts.

Puppets—both artistic and traditional

Havelská Market—gifts and people-watching

The most famous and expensive brand is Moser, located in the mall at Na Příkopě 12 (and other branches around town). A number of glass shops are along Celetná street.

Garnets and Beads: For centuries, the blood-red gemstones mined near Prague supplied Europe's jewelers. Ask for a certificate of authenticity to avoid a glass fake. A *"granát Turnov"* label indicates quality. You'll find several jewelry stores on Dlouhá street (branching off the Old Town Square), including Turnov Granát Co-op (at Dlouhá 28). You'll also see costume jewelry *(bižutérie)* sold everywhere, especially local glass beads by the Jablonex brand.

Art Nouveau: Look for glassware, home decor, linens, posters, and other items. Near (or in) the Municipal House are three good stores: Modernista is downstairs inside. Artěl is at Celetná 29, a block west of the Municipal House (www.artelglass.com). Kubista is inside the House of the Black Madonna (Ovocný Trh 19, www.kubista.cz).

Other Fun Souvenir Ideas: Old-fashioned porcelain (traditional blue-on-white), images of the kids' character "Krtek," the brain-teasing puzzle "hedgehog in the cage" *(ježek v kleci),* the sardine-shaped pocket-knife ("fishlet"), and "kitchen witch" good-luck dolls.

What Not to Buy: Stacking dolls, fur hats, amber, vodka flasks, and other Russian souvenirs—these are most definitely not Czech.

Getting a VAT Refund: If you purchase more than 2,001 Kč (about $100) worth of goods at a single store, you may be eligible to get a refund of the 21 percent Value-Added Tax (VAT). Have the store fill out the paperwork. At the airport, get your papers stamped by customs *before* going through security. (At Václav Havel Airport, customs for Terminal 1 is in the far left-hand corner of the departure hall, next to the oversize baggage desk. At Terminal 2, customs is immediately to the right of the security check.) You can cash in your refund on the spot (less a service fee) at a Travelex office located near customs. Get more details from your merchant or see ricksteves.com/vat.

Customs for American Shoppers: You are allowed to take home $800 worth of items per person duty-free, once every 30 days. You can also bring in duty-free a liter of alcohol. As for food, you can take home many processed and packaged foods (e.g., vacuum-packed cheeses, chocolate) but no fresh produce or meats. Any liquid-containing foods must be packed in checked luggage, a potential recipe for disaster. To check customs rules and duty rates, visit help.cbp.gov.

Practicalities

Nightlife

For many, just strolling the streets or enjoying a drink in a view spot makes for their evening entertainment. But Prague also booms with live and inexpensive theater, classical music, jazz, and pop entertainment.

Information: Everything is listed in several monthly cultural events programs (free at TIs) and in the Prague Post newspaper (60 Kč at newsstands, www.praguepost.com). The best one-stop-shopping place to see what's on today and tomorrow and buy tickets is the Via Musica box office. The handy event schedule is posted on the wall. There are two branches: Next to Týn Church on the Old Town Square (daily 10:30-19:30, tel. 224-826-969, www.viamusica.cz) and in the Little Quarter across from the Church of St. Nicholas (daily 10:30-18:00, tel. 257-535-568). Another ticket outlet—for the serious concert venues and most music clubs—is Ticketpro (reservations tel. 296-329-999, www.ticketpro.cz). Locals dress up for the more serious concerts, opera, and ballet, though tourists are fine wearing casual clothes (still, avoid shorts, sneakers, or flip-flops).

Classical Music: Almost any day of the week you can choose from a half-dozen classical music concerts performed in a delightful Old World setting with crowd-pleasing music. They often feature works by three composers with ties to Prague: Mozart, who lived here during his prime; Antonín Dvořák, who built an international career in symphonic music based on Czech folk tunes; and Bedřich Smetana, who wrote a stirring work about the Vltava River (The Moldau). Concerts typically run around 600 Kč and last about an hour.

For top-notch classical music (September through June), take in the Prague Symphony Orchestra (box office outside Municipal House, tel. 222-002-336, www.fok.cz, pokladna@fok.cz) or the Czech Philharmonic (box office at Alšovo nábřeží 12, tel. 227-059-352, www.ceskafilharmonie.cz). For opera and ballet, the best-known company is the National Theater (tel. 224-912-673, www.narodni-divadlo.cz). Prague hosts several world-class classical and jazz music festivals from May to September. Get details at: www.festival.cz, www.pragueproms.cz, www.dvorakovapraha.cz, and www.agharta.cz.

Black Light Theater: This is Prague's most unique form of entertainment—you'll see it advertised everywhere. These playful, absurd performances got their start in Prague in the 1960s. The performers wear fluorescent costumes that glow under ultraviolet black lights. Since it's mostly pantomimed or danced, there's no language barrier. It's definitely

Top-notch classical music is everywhere.

The pub is the Czech center of nightlife.

an unusual theater experience, and most people are glad they've done it… once. Of the many theaters, try Ta Fantastika (performing their poetic classic, *Aspects of Alice,* near Charles Bridge at Karlova 8, tel. 222-221-366, www.tafantastika.cz) or Image Theater (more slapstick, near Old Town Square at Pařížská 4, tel. 222-314-448, www.imagetheatre.cz).

Live Music: It thrives. That's particularly true for rock bands and singer-songwriter folk music, but also jazz and ethnic. Clubs are intimate (100-200 people), with decades of tradition. Music starts around 21:00, with a cover charge around 100-250 Kč. Later at night, the scene might transform to a DJ and dancing. You can buy tickets at the door or from their website, or from Ticketpro (www.ticketpro.cz). Venerable clubs include the Roxy (near Old Town Square at Dlouhá 33, tel. 224-826-296, easy to book at www.roxy.cz); the Agharta Jazz Club (near Old Town Square at Železná 16, tel. 222-211-275, www.agharta.cz); the Lucerna Music Bar (bottom of Wenceslas Square in Lucerna Arcade Mall at Vodičkova 36, tel. 224-217-108, www.musicbar.cz); and the communist-era classic Malostranská Beseda (in Little Quarter at Malostranské Náměstí 21, tel. 257-409-123, www.malostranska-beseda.cz).

The best place to buy music by Czech musicians (classical or contemporary) is the Bontonland CD and video store, at the bottom of Wenceslas Square (inside the mall with the big Kenvelo sign).

Earplug Alert: Prague—with its cheap beer and easy fun—can seem like a rolling frat, stag, or hen party into the wee hours. You're warned.

TOURS IN PRAGUE

Guided Group Tours: A staggering number of small companies offer walking tours for groups of tourists—you'll see ads everywhere. You can easily join on the spot and probably get a hardworking young guide at a good price. Try showing up at the Astronomical Clock a couple of minutes before 8:00, 10:00, or 11:00, chat with the umbrella-holding guides, and choose one you click with. Many offer "free" tours, which aren't really free because you're expected to tip (with paper bills rather than a few chintzy coins). Also, the TI at the Old Town Square offers quality three-hour group tours.

Private Guides: Hiring your own personal guide in Prague is particularly smart—they're twice as helpful for half the price of guides in Western Europe. Prices run about 1,000 Kč for a two-hour tour for a small group. Comparison-shop the following companies' websites to see what they offer, and make arrangements by email:

Personal Prague Guide Service has personable and knowledgeable guides (mobile 777-225-205, www.personalpragueguide.com, sarka@me.com). PragueWalker is friendly and enthusiastic about history (mobile 603-181-300, www.praguewalker.com). Jana Hronková has an unstuffy

"Free" walking tours indicate a trend—it's a buyer's market (but expect to tip).

style and a penchant for the Jewish Quarter (mobile 732-185-180, www. experience-prague.info). Martin Bělohradský loves art, architecture, and chemistry (mobile 723-414-565, martinb5666@gmail.com). Jana Krátká shares 20th-century history (mobile 776-571-538, janapragueguide@ gmail.com). Taste Local Beer does microbrew pub crawls (www.taste localbeer.com). Kamil and Petra Vondrouš are especially helpful for driving day trips from Prague (mobile 605-701-861, www.prague-extra.com, info@ prague-extra.com). For a list of more guides, see www.guide-prague.cz.

Bus Tours: Since Prague's sightseeing core is not accessible by bus, I can't recommend any of the city's bus tour companies, not even the hop-on, hop-off bus tours that work so well in many other European cities. Bus tours do make sense for day trips out of Prague (see page 136).

Ricksteves.com

This Pocket Guide is one of dozens of titles in my series of guidebooks on European travel. I also produce a public television series, *Rick Steves' Europe,* and a public radio show, *Travel with Rick Steves.* My website, ricksteves.com, offers a wealth of free travel information, including videos and podcasts of my shows, travel forums, guidebook updates, my travel blog, and my guide to European rail passes—plus an online travel store and information on our tours of Europe.

Rick Steves Audio Europe App: This free app makes it easy for you to download my audio tours of many of Europe's top attractions. For this book, I have an audio tour of the Prague City Walk. The app also offers many insightful travel interviews from my public radio show with experts from around the globe. You can download the free app via Apple's App Store, Google Play, or the Amazon Appstore. For more info, see www. ricksteves.com/audioeurope.

How Was Your Trip? If you'd like to share your tips, concerns, and discoveries after using this book, please fill out the survey at Ricksteves. com/feedback. It helps us and fellow travelers.

Czech Survival Phrases

Hello. (formal)	**Dobrý den.**	DOH-bree dehn
Hi. / Bye. (informal)	**Ahoj.**	AH-hoy
Do you speak English?	**Mluvíte anglicky?**	MLOO-vee-teh ANG-lits-kee
Yes. / No.	**Ano. / Ne.**	AH-noh / neh
I don't understand.	**Nerozumím.**	NEH-roh-zoo-meem
Please. / You're welcome. / Can I help you?	**Prosím.**	PROH-seem
Thank you.	**Děkuji.**	DYACK-kwee
Excuse me. / I'm sorry.	**Promiňte.**	PROH-meen-teh
(No) problem.	**(To není) problém.**	(toh NEH-nee) proh-BLEHM
Good.	**Dobře.**	DOHB-zhay
Goodbye.	**Nashledanou.**	NAH-skleh-dah-noh
one / two	**jeden / dva**	YAY-dehn / dvah
three / four	**tři / čtyři**	tzhee / CHTEE-zhee
five / six	**pět / šest**	pyeht / shehst
seven / eight	**sedm / osm**	SEH-dum / OH-sum
nine / ten	**devět / deset**	DEHV-yeht / DHE-seht
hundred / thousand	**sto / tisíc**	stoh / TEE-seets
How much?	**Kolik?**	KOH-leek
local currency	**koruna (Kč)**	koh-ROO-nah
Write it?	**Napište to?**	NAH-pish-teh toh
Is it free?	**Je to zadarmo?**	yeh toh ZAH-dar-moh
Is it included?	**Je to v ceně?**	yeh tohf TSAY-nyeh
Where can I find / buy...?	**Kde mohu najít / koupit...?**	gday MOH-hoo NAH-yeet / KOH-pit
We'd like...	**Rádi bychom...**	RAH-dyee BEE-khohm
...a room.	**...pokoj.**	POH-koy
...a ticket to ___. (destination)	**...jízdenka do ___.**	YEEZ-dehn-kah doh ___
Is it possible?	**Je to možné?**	yeh toh MOHZH-neh
Where is...?	**Kde je...?**	gday yeh
...the train station	**...nádraží**	NAH-drah-zhee
...the bus station	**...autobusové nádraží**	OW-toh-boo-soh-veh NAH-drah-zhee
...the tourist information office	**...turistická informační kancelář**	TOO-rih-stit-skah EEN-for-mahch-nee KAHN-tseh-lahzh
...the toilet	**...vécé**	VEHT-seh
men / women	**muži / ženy**	MOO-zhee / ZHAY-nee
left / right	**vlevo / vpravo**	VLEH-voh / FPRAH-voh
straight	**rovně**	ROHV-nyeh
At what time...?	**V kolik...?**	FKOH-leek
...does this open/close	**...otevírají / zavírají**	OH-teh-vee-rah-yee / ZAH-vee-rah-yee
Just a moment, please.	**Moment, prosím.**	MOH-mehnt PROH-seem
now / soon / later	**teď / brzy / později**	tedge / BIR-zih / POHZH-dyeh-yee
today / tomorrow	**dnes / zítra**	duh-NEHS / ZEE-trah

In the Restaurant

We'd like to reserve...	**Rádi bychom zarezervovali...**	RAH-dyee BEE-khohm ZAH-reh-zehr-voh-vah-lee
...a table for one / two.	**...stůl pro jednoho / dva.**	stool proh YEHD-noh-hoh / dvah
non-smoking	**nekuřácký**	NEH-kuhzh-aht-skee
Is this table free?	**Je tento stůl volný?**	yeh TEHN-toh stool VOHL-nee
The menu (in English), please.	**Jídelní lístek (v angličtině), prosím.**	YEE-dehl-nee LEE-stehk (FAHN-gleech-tee-nyeh) PROH-seem
service included	**spropitné je zahrnuto**	SPROH-pit-neh yeh ZAH-har-noo-toh
service not included	**spropitné není zahrnuto**	SPROH-pit-neh NEH-nee ZAH-har-noo-toh
cover charge	**kuvert**	KOO-vert
"to go"	**s sebou**	SEH-boh
daily special	**denní nabídka**	DEH-nyee nah-BEET-kah
appetizers	**předkrm**	PZHEHD-krim
bread / cheese	**chléb / sýr**	khlehb/ seer
sandwich	**sendvič**	SEHND-vich
soup / salad	**polévka / salát**	poh-LEHV-kah / SAH-laht
meat / poultry	**maso / drůbež**	MAH-soh / DROO-behzh
fish / seafood	**ryby / mořské plody**	RIH-bih / MOHZH-skeh PLOH-dih
fruit / vegetables	**ovoce / zelenina**	OH-voht-seh / ZEH-leh-nyee-nah
dessert	**dezert**	DEH-zehrt
(tap) water	**voda (z kohoutku)**	VOH-dah (SKOH-hoht-koo)
mineral water	**minerální voda**	MIH-neh-rahl-nyee VOH-dah
carbonated / not carbonated	**s bublinkami / bez bublinek**	SBOOB-leen-kah-mee / behz BOO-blee-nehk
milk	**mléko**	MLEH-koh
(orange) juice	**(pomerančový) džus**	(POH-mehr-ahn-choh-vee) "juice"
coffee / tea	**káva / čaj**	KAH-vah / chai
wine	**víno**	VEE-noh
red / white	**červené / bílé**	CHEHR-veh-neh / BEE-leh
glass / bottle	**sklenka / lahev**	SKLEHN-kah / LAH-hehv
beer	**pivo**	PEE-voh
light / dark	**světlé / tmavé**	SVYEHT-leh / TMAH-veh
vodka	**vodka**	VOHD-kah
Cheers!	**Na zdraví!**	nah zdrah-VEE
Enjoy your meal.	**Dobrou chuť.**	DOH-broh khoot
More. / Another.	**Více / Další.**	VEET-seh / DAHL-shee
The same.	**To samé.**	toh SAH-meh
The bill, please.	**Účet, prosím.**	OO-cheht PROH-seem
I'll pay.	**Zaplatím.**	ZAH-plah-teem
tip	**spropitné**	SPROH-pit-neh
Delicious!	**Výborné!**	VEE-bohr-neh

INDEX

Start your trip at

Our website enhances this book and turns

Explore Europe

At ricksteves.com you can browse through thousands of articles, videos, photos and radio interviews, plus find a wealth of money-saving travel tips for planning your dream trip. And with our mobile-friendly website, you can easily access all this great travel information anywhere you go.

TV Shows

Preview the places you'll visit by watching entire half-hour episodes of Rick Steves' Europe (choose from all 100 shows) on-demand, for free.

ricksteves.com

your travel dreams into affordable reality

Radio Interviews

Enjoy ready access to Rick's vast library of radio interviews covering

travel tips and cultural insights that relate specifically to your Europe travel plans.

Travel Forums

Learn, ask, share! Our online community of savvy travelers is a great resource for first-time travelers to Europe, as well as seasoned pros. You'll find forums on each country, plus travel tips and restaurant/hotel reviews. You can even ask one of our well-traveled staff to chime in with an opinion.

Travel News

Subscribe to our free Travel News e-newsletter, and get monthly updates from Rick on what's happening in Europe.

Audio Europe™

Rick's Free Travel App

Get your FREE Rick Steves Audio Europe™ app to enjoy…

- Dozens of self-guided tours of Europe's top museums, sights and historic walks

- Hundreds of tracks filled with cultural insights and sightseeing tips from Rick's radio interviews

- All organized into handy geographic playlists

- For Apple and Android

With Rick whispering in your ear, Europe gets even better.

Find out more at ricksteves.com

Pack Light and Right

Gear up for your next adventure at ricksteves.com

Light Luggage

Pack light and right with Rick Steves' affordable, custom-designed rolling carry-on bags, backpacks, day packs and shoulder bags.

Accessories

From packing cubes to moneybelts and beyond, Rick has personally selected the travel goodies that will help your trip go smoother.

Rick Steves has

Experience maximum Europe

Save time and energy

This guidebook is your independent-travel toolkit. But for all it delivers, it's still up to you to devote the time and energy it takes to manage the preparation and logistics that are essential for a happy trip. If that's a hassle, there's a solution.

Rick Steves Tours

A Rick Steves tour takes you to Europe's most interesting places with great guides and small groups

great tours, too!

with minimum stress

of 28 or less. We follow Rick's favorite itineraries, ride in comfy buses, stay in family-run hotels, and bring you intimately close to the Europe you've traveled so far to see. Most importantly, we take away the logistical headaches so you can focus on the fun.

Join the fun

This year we'll take 18,000 free-spirited travelers—nearly half of them repeat customers—along with us on 40 different itineraries, from Ireland to Italy to Istanbul. Is a Rick Steves tour the right fit for your travel dreams? Find out at ricksteves.com, where you can also get Rick's latest tour catalog and free Tour Experience DVD.

Europe is best experienced with happy travel partners. We hope you can join us.

BEST OF GUIDES

Best of France
Best of Germany
Best of Ireland
Best of Italy
Best of Spain

EUROPE GUIDES

Best of Europe
Eastern Europe
Europe Through the Back Door
Mediterranean Cruise Ports
Northern European Cruise Ports

COUNTRY GUIDES

Croatia & Slovenia
England
France
Germany
Great Britain
Ireland
Italy
Portugal
Scandinavia
Scotland
Spain
Switzerland

CITY & REGIONAL GUIDES

Amsterdam & the Netherlands
Belgium: Bruges, Brussels, Antwerp & Ghent
Barcelona
Budapest
Florence & Tuscany
Greece: Athens & the Peloponnese
Istanbul
London
Paris
Prague & the Czech Republic
Provence & the French Riviera
Rome
Venice
Vienna, Salzburg & Tirol

SNAPSHOT GUIDES

Basque Country: Spain & France
Berlin
Copenhagen & the Best of Denmark
Dublin
Dubrovnik
Hill Towns of Central Italy
Italy's Cinque Terre
Krakow, Warsaw & Gdansk
Lisbon
Loire Valley

Maximize your travel skills with a good guidebook.

Madrid & Toledo
Milan & the Italian Lakes District
Naples & the Amalfi Coast
Northern Ireland
Norway
Sevilla, Granada & Southern Spain
St. Petersburg, Helsinki & Tallinn
Stockholm

POCKET GUIDES

Amsterdam
Athens
Barcelona
Florence
London
Munich & Salzburg
Paris
Prague
Rome
Venice
Vienna

TRAVEL CULTURE

Europe 101
European Christmas
Postcards from Europe
Travel as a Political Act

RICK STEVES' EUROPE DVDs

12 New Shows 2015-2016
Austria & the Alps
The Complete Collection 2000-2016
Eastern Europe

England & Wales
European Christmas
European Travel Skills & Specials
France
Germany, BeNeLux & More
Greece, Turkey & Portugal
The Holy Land: Israelis & Palestinians Today
Iran
Ireland & Scotland
Italy's Cities
Italy's Countryside
Scandinavia
Spain
Travel Extras

PHRASE BOOKS & DICTIONARIES

French
French, Italian & German
German
Italian
Portuguese
Spanish

PLANNING MAPS

Britain, Ireland & London
Europe
France & Paris
Germany, Austria & Switzerland
Ireland
Italy
Spain & Portugal

RickSteves.com 🅕🅣 @RickSteves

Rick Steves books are available at bookstores and through online booksellers.

Photo © Patricia Feaster

PHOTO CREDITS

Avalon Travel
a member of the Perseus Books Group
1700 Fourth Street
Berkeley, CA 94710

Text © 2016 by Rick Steves' Europe
All rights reserved.
Maps © 2016 by Rick Steves' Europe. All rights reserved.
Printed in China by RR Donnelley
First printing July 2016

ISBN 978-1-61238-498-6
ISSN 2469-455X

For the latest on Rick's lectures, guidebooks, tours, public radio show, and public television series, contact Rick Steves' Europe, 130 Fourth Avenue North, Edmonds, WA 98020, tel. 425/771-8303, fax 425/771-0833, ricksteves.com, rick@ricksteves.com.

Rick Steves' Europe
Special Publications Manager: Risa Laib
Managing Editor: Jennifer Madison Davis
Editors: Glenn Eriksen, Tom Griffin, Katherine Gustafson, Suzanne Kotz, Cathy Lu, Carrie Shepherd
Editorial & Production Assistant: Jessica Shaw
Researchers: Cameron Hewitt, Gene Openshaw
Maps & Graphics: David C. Hoerlein, Sandra Hundacker, Lauren Mills, Mary Rostad

Avalon Travel
Senior Editor and Series Manager: Madhu Prasher
Editor: Jamie Andrade
Associate Editor: Sierra Machado
Copy Editor: Judith Brown
Proofreader: Kelly Lydick
Indexer: Stephen Callahan
Production & Typesetting: McGuire Barber Design
Cover Design: Kimberly Glyder Design
Interior Design: Darren Alessi
Cover Photo: View of Old Town from Charles Bridge © Martin Molcan | Dreamstime.com
Maps & Graphics: Kat Bennett, Mike Morgenfeld

ABOUT THE AUTHORS

Rick Steves

Since 1973, Rick has spent 100 days every year exploring Europe. Along with writing best-selling guidebooks, Rick produces a public television series *(Rick Steves' Europe)*, a public radio show *(Travel with Rick Steves)*, a blog (on Facebook), and an app and podcast *(Rick Steves Audio Europe)*; writes a syndicated newspaper column; organizes tours that take 20,000 travelers to Europe annually; and offers an info-packed website (Ricksteves.com). With the help of his hardworking staff of 100 at Rick Steves' Europe—in Edmonds, just north of Seattle—Rick's mission is to make European travel fun, affordable, and culturally enlightening for Americans.

Connect with Rick: 🆕 facebook.com/RickSteves   🐦 twitter: @RickSteves
📷 instagram: ricksteveseurope

Honza Vihan

Honza Vihan grew up roaming the Czech countryside in search of the Wild West. Once the borders opened, he set off for South Dakota. His journey took him to China, Honduras, India, and Iran, where he contributed to several travel guides. Honza lives in Prague with his family, teaches Chinese, and leads Rick Steves' tours through Eastern Europe.

Gene Openshaw, Contributor

Gene has co-authored a dozen Rick Steves books and contributes to many others. For this book, he wrote material on Europe's art, history, and contemporary culture. When not traveling, Gene enjoys composing music, recovering from his 1973 trip to Europe with Rick, and living everyday life with his daughter.

FOLDOUT COLOR MAP

The foldout map on the opposite page includes:

• A map of Prague on one side
• Greater Prague and Public Transportation maps on the other side